Assu of Cape Mudge

*arry Assu and Joy Inglis at the First
lmon Ceremony, Cape Mudge, May
84. Photograph by Hilary Stewart.
e blanket worn by Joy Inglis was
esented to her on this occasion with
e words "Now you are one of us."
ra Cook designed the crest of Whale
at appears of the back of the Assu
ankets. Louisa Assu made the
anket, with the assistance of Pearl
ick, who sewed the buttons. Later in
e same year at Harry Assu's potlatch,
y Inglis received the name
xkalaǧa (lots of fire) for her work
genereal with Native people, thus
ating her to Harry Assu and his
tended family.*

Harry Assu, a chief of the Lekwiltok – the southernmost tribe of the Kwagiulth Nation – was born in 1905 in Cape Mudge, Quadra Island, British Columbia. His father was Billy Assu, a renowned chief of the Northwest Coast, who led his people from a rich traditional way of life into modern prosperity.

As well as being a family chronicle, Harry Assu's recollections tell the little-known story of the Lekwiltok from legendary times to the present. Drawing on the oral traditions of his people, he narrates the story of the "Great Flood" which gives sacred sanction to territories settled by them. Hand-drawn and historical maps illustrate his account of coastal alliances over the last two centuries and provide an understanding of the current land and sea claims of the Kwagiulth Nation.

Supernatural beings inhabited the worlds of his ancestors and of Assu's boyhood, and he recalls encounters with birds and whales which held particular significance for his family. His description of a more recent experience – his own potlatch in 1984 – is perhaps the most complete record of the order of events in a modern potlatch. As well, his account of the seizure of potlatch regalia in 1922, the jailing of the leaders, and the subsequent restoration of these family treasures is a rare view from inside Indian culture.

Harry Assu put his faith in education and welcomed the efforts of teachers sent by the Methodist Missionary Society. He remains an elder and supporter of the United Church at Cape Mudge. Symbolizing the achievement of his tribe in bringing into harmony a traditional culture with commercial fishing, in which he was involved for sixty years, Harry Assu reminisces about the old cannery days on the coast and tells of the continuing struggle by his people to maintain a place in the modern fishing industry.

Assu of Cape Mudge is illustrated with drawings of supernatural events by artist and author Hilary Stewart which were drawn in the vicinity of Cape Mudge while Harry Assu described these dramatic occurrences. The Kwakwala words have been transcribed by Peter Wilson, with a full record of language association, meaning, and optional spellings from different sources. Also included in the book and of general interest are an appendix of ancient tales by the Lekwiltok and a genealogical chart of the Assu family.

This personal memoir by an important native leader of British Columbia will delight anthropologists, historians, and all those with an interest in native studies and autobiography.

HARRY ASSU was the first elected Chief Councillor of the We-Wai-Kai band at Cape Mudge, where he still resides. He continues to promote preservation of the Kwagiulth traditions he learned in his youth.

JOY INGLIS is a specialist in coastal Indian culture, with a particular interest in the art, myth, and ceremony of the Kwagiulth Nation. She has lived on Quadra Island since 1974 and frequently teaches continuing education courses.

Assu of Cape Mudge

Recollections of a
Coastal Indian Chief
Harry Assu with Joy Inglis

University of British Columbia Press
Vancouver 1989

© The University of British Columbia Press 1989
All rights reserved
Printed in Canada
ISBN 0-7748-0333-9 (cloth)
        0-7748-0341-X (paper)

Printed on acid free paper

Canadian Cataloguing in Publication Data
Assu, Harry, 1905–
  Assu of Cape Mudge

  Bibliography: p.
  Includes index.
  ISBN 0-7748-0333-9 (bound). – ISBN 0-7748-0341-X
(pbk.)

  1. Assu, Harry, 1905–   2. Kwakiutl Indians
– Biography. 3. Indians of North America – British
Columbia – Cape Mudge – Biography. 4. Assu family.
5. Cape Mudge (B.C.) – Genealogy. 6. Kwakiutl Indians
– Genealogy. 7. Indians of North America – British
Columbia – Cape Mudge – Genealogy. I. Inglis, Joy,
1919–   II.Title.
E99.K9A88 1989   971.1'00497   C89-091375-7

This book has been published with the help of grants from the Canada Council, the British Columbia
Heritage Trust, and private sources.

University of British Columbia Press
6344 Memorial Rd
Vancouver, B.C. V6T 1W5

Contents

Maps and Illustrations

Figures

Abbreviations

BCAA   B.C. Conference Archives. United Church. Vancouver, B.C.

CMC   Canadian Museum of Civilization. Ottawa

CRMA   Campbell River Museum and Archives. Campbell River, B.C.

KM   Kwagiulth Museum. Cape Mudge, B.C.

MAI   Museum of the American Indian. New York

MOA   Museum of Anthropology. University of British Columbia

NMM   National Anthropological Archives. Museum of Natural History, Smit sonian Institution. Washington, D.C.

PABC   Provincial Archives of British Columbia. Victoria, B.C.

RBCM   Royal British Columbia Museum. Victoria

UBCL   Library of the University of British Columbia. Special Collectio Vancouver

VM   Vancouver Museum.

VPL   Vancouver Public Library. Historical Photographs Section

Foreword

When Europeans first settled in this country they not only took lands from the aboriginal peoples but also took them out of their own histories. History was written from the point of view of the newcomers, who referred to themselves as explorers, pioneers, and founders of civilization. The contributions of the First Nations were coincidentally marginalized or relegated to a "prehistory" that was also controlled by the colonizers. What Chief Harry Assu has done with this book is to bring history back to his own people.

It is controversial, for Mr. Assu speaks frankly and personally about serious and important issues such as colonial oppression, discrimination, land disputes, aboriginal rights, and the bureaucratic machinations of governmental agencies. It is also a liberating story because it places Indians back into the picture as active agents who make as well as report their histories and who therefore are taking charge of their own destinies. Asserting control over one's own history is thus an important act of self-determination. Historians empower and history is empowering. Mr. Assu also demonstrates through his own life's work how it is possible and important to retain a strong Indian identity while integrating successfully in the wider society.

Joy Inglis is surely a most appropriate person to work with Mr. Assu. She has been student of Kwagiulth culture for over thirty years and is a long time resident of the area, a personal friend of the Assu family, and a sensitive recorder. And Hilary Stewart has added her renowned artistry. Both have devoted their careers to studying and teaching and contribute much here (as they have elsewhere) to the repatriation of Indian history. It is an honour to add a foreword commending such a useful study. I have had the privilege of experiencing the traditional Kwagiulth hospitality of Mr. Assu and his family and have always admired the work and spirit of Inglis and Stewart, whom I have known for many years.

Michael M. Ames, Director
Museum of Anthropology, The University of British Columbia

Acknowledgments

We are grateful to our families who through the years this work was underway heartened us by believing that our work was worthwhile. Special thanks to Audrey Wilson and Mary Clifton, Lisa Wells and Frank Sheran, who helped with genealogy; Don and Louisa Assu and Stephen and Cissy Assu, who read early drafts of the manuscript and provided us with photographs; and to Flora and James Sewid, Agnes Alfred, and Dora Cook, who discussed with us family ceremonial events including the potlatch described in Chapter 7; and to Daisy Sewid-Smith, who arranged for typing notes of these joint sessions and was available to us for consultation on matters requiring clarification. We also want to thank Erica Claus and Stephen Inglis, who from time to time were consulted on the form of presentation of the book; and Bob Inglis, whose loving encouragement never flagged through the years the book was being written. We deeply appreciate the backing of Stephen, Mel, and Don Assu and families, who affirmed and supported our work at all times, and that of Rod Naknakim, who helped us with legal services and read from the manuscript for us on the occasion of a pre-publication literary event. Many thanks to Mark Henderson of Campbell River for the right to publish the photograph of his painting "Southeast Wind" as shown in association with a We-Wai-Kum tale in Appendix Six.

We are pleased indeed that Michael Ames, Director of the Museum of Anthropology, University of British Columbia, has written the foreword to this book. Many researchers and scholars in anthropology have shared their expertise with us. Wayne Suttles read the manuscript in its early form and encouraged our efforts. We acknowledge with pleasure the help of Jay Powell for critiquing the manuscript and giving us valuable suggestions and Dorothy Kennedy and Randy Bouchard, who offered the research resources of the B.C. Indian Language Project to us and read the manuscript through its several drafts to our benefit. Mari Mauzé has exchanged information and ideas with us over the years. Joan Zamluck was kind enough to proofread the first drafts of early chapters of the book. Ruby Wilson and Alberta and Dan Billy of Cape Mudge have contributed photographs and documents which we gratefully acknowledge.

We have been fortunate to have the assistance of linguist Peter Wilson, who developed an orthographic rendering of words in the native language which contain sounds not made in English. The renderings in this book are of liqʷala, a dialect of Kwakwala spoken by the Lekwiltok. We wish to thank Peter for his work with us and for giving final form to the linguistic presentation in this book.

We wish to express the gratification we feel in our association with David Stouck for his enthusiasm for our undertaking and for proofreading the manuscript before recommending the work for publication.

Special hearty thanks to Hilary Stewart, artist and author, who spent valuable time with us photographing for the book, depicting ritual occasions of ethnographic interest on site while the associated stories were related, preparing sketches from faded photographs, working on maps and drawing illustrations to adorn the book. We also acknowledge with pleasure the work of artist-photographer John Gordon of Campbell River and others who supplied us with photographic materials.

Museums, art galleries, libraries, and archives have assisted us with information and documentation. We are especially beholden to the Kwagiulth Museum at Cape Mudge and the Campbell River Museum and Archives for their co-operative assistance. Bob Stewart of B.C. Conference Archives, United Church of Canada, gave of his voluntary time and expertise. Peter Macnair of the Royal British Columbia Museum identified and verified photographs of museum artifacts.

We wish to thank Hilda Gallagher, that gallant lady who has taken the manuscript through its seemingly endless revisions on the word processer. She has been a trusted companion in the production of the work. The encouragement of all our friends has sustained us.

The following agencies have provided funds for underwriting the cost of producing the manuscript: The Leon and Thea Koerner Foundation, The Cape Mudge Band, School District 72, for secretarial work and computer time, B.C. Packers Ltd., Kwagiulth Museum, and Canada Council (Explorations). We are happy to acknowledge their assistance and thank them for their support.

Introduction

The Indian village of Cape Mudge is located on the southern tip of Quadra Island, directly across from Campbell River on Vancouver Island. It is the major village of the We-Wai-Kai band, part of British Columbia's Kwagiulth Nation. Toward the close of the nineteenth century, the people of Cape Mudge chose as their leader Billy Assu (1867–1965), a man of superior physical strength, who, through his sound practical wisdom and great skill in speaking, became one of the most renowned and respected chiefs of the Northwest Coast. During his lifetime, he led an aboriginal people from a traditional order into prosperous modernity. This book is the history of the Assu family and of Cape Mudge and associated villages as told by Harry Assu, only living son of Billy Assu, who in 1954 succeeded his father as first elected chief councillor of the We-Wai-Kai band at Cape Mudge, a position in which he served for sixteen years.

Harry Assu symbolizes the achievement of the Indians at Cape Mudge in harmonizing the rich traditional culture of the Kwagiulth Indians with life in the commercial fishing industry in which he was involved for over sixty years. He is foremost in giving ceremonial feasts and potlatches at Cape Mudge. Harry Assu is also founding board member of the Nuyumbalees Society, which operates the Kwagiulth Museum on the reserve. At the same time, he is an elder of the Quadra Island United Church at Cape Mudge and a member of the Campbell River Shrine Lodge of the Masonic Order at Campbell River. He has been a lifelong member of the Native Brotherhood, an association representing Indian fishing interests, and keeps in touch with the federal Department of Fisheries and Oceans by discussions on behalf of his people. He receives visiting dignitaries at Cape Mudge and acts as spokesperson in cultural exchanges with other nations.

Harry Assu dedicates his autobiography to his distinguished father, Chief Billy Assu, who initiated the process that has led to the success of his people in two worlds. In the first two decades of this century Chief Billy Assu enhanced the reputation of his people in potlatching with wealth brought in from the newly established commercial fishing industry, but he also helped them adapt to changing circumstances, urging them to build up the fishing fleet and engage in logging enterprises, thus securing every possible advantage for his village in a world rapidly encroaching on traditional ways. Throughout this book Harry Assu relates episodes in which his farsighted father played a part, thus adding to our knowledge of an important early coastal chief with first-hand information from his son.

In his narrative, Harry Assu offers an unusual perspective which reveals his place in the universe yet draws upon the shared experiences of his people, the We-Wai-Kai. It is a view from inside his culture and consequently significant in terms of the growing demand by Indians in Canada and cultural minorities or "indigenous peoples" throughout the world to speak for themselves. Harry Assu's account is a unique contribution because references to the Lekwiltok tribe, of which the We-Wai-Kai of Cape Mudge are a part, are not readily accessible in scholarly literature. Until the publication of this work the Lekwiltok tribe of the Kwagiulth Nation at Cape Mudge have not had a native interpreter of their own history.

What is known to the outside world of the traditions of the Kwagiulth people before European contact is largely derived from the great body of published research findings by Franz Boas, who began his work on the B.C. Coast as early as 1880 and continued to produce information on Kwagiulth culture for over forty years, assisted by George Hunt, a native of the village of Fort Rupert on the northern part of Vancouver Island. This focus somewhat obscures cultural differences that developed in other Kwagiulth villages of the time, scattered as they were over great distances on islands and in inlets on the Mainland and in some cases bordering on peoples of different languages and cultures. Harry Assu speaks as a Lekwiltok, whose territory put the tribe in long and continuous association with the Island-Comox speakers of the Northern Coast Salish people.

At some time in the mid-eighteenth century, prior to European contact with the Kwagiulth by Captain George Vancouver in 1792, the Lekwiltok bands moved south into the northern Strait of Georgia, occupying territory previously held by the Northern Coast Salish. It was a this time that the We-Wai-Kai of Cape Mudge founded their village of Tekya in Topaze Harbour that became central to their origin story and other bands of the Lekwiltok occupied villages still farther south along the Mainland. On Vancouver Island the Lekwiltok allied themselves with one branch of the Salish, the Island-Comox speakers in their high-ranking village at Salmon River in Kelsey Bay. With their Comox allies, Lekwiltok war parties raided the lesser Island-Comox villages southward, including those beside the Campbell River, eventually establishing a village there, at Cape Mudge, and at Comox on Courtenay Bay.

From Cape Mudge the We-Wai-Kai and the Comox launched raids farther south on Vancouver Island, in Puget Sound, and upriver on the Fraser, where they struck twice at the Hudson's Bay fort at Langley. These conflicts have been dramatized in newspaper and magazine accounts of the history of Cape Mudge, but without recognizing the co-operative aspects of Lekwiltok–Island-Comox relations as emphasized by Harry Assu – the reality of which is attested to by the complete assimilation of the two groups today.

Chief Harry Assu is in his eighties now. Fortunately, his memory serves him well, and his recall of dates is exceptional. His knowledge of events before his lifetime is drawn from the oral tradition of his people and particularly from the teachings of his father and maternal grandfather. What he presents is in substantial accord with notes by researchers, most of whom consulted his father as their main respondent; but where differences in interpretation of historical events do occur, they have been footnoted so that other sources may be consulted.

Harry Assu holds in mind the nurturing relationship between humankind and other populations of animals that is part of the traditional Indian system of thought. On several occasions, especially in the early chapters of the book, he recalls instances of interaction with birds and whales that have particular significance for him and for his family. Whale is an important crest of the Assu family, figuring on their memorial poles and on ceremonial robes. By relating instances of unusual contact with whales, he affirms the affinity of his family to the powerful being displayed as a family crest. The spectacular performances in the potlatches described by Harry Assu in the last chapter express the dramatic encounters in the past between these powerful and dangerous creatures of the supernatural world and the ancestors who bravely sought their powers.

Throughout his narrative, Harry Assu weaves the strands of family history that validate position, great names, and rights to crests and ritual performances that are the part of the treasured wealth of Kwagiulth families passed down through time by heredity and marriage. These rights are jealously guarded and hotly contested by families claiming them, particularly by those people involved in the potlatch today. Contending with one another is an integral part of the complex process of the potlatch, and disputes are to be expected. Throughout this book Harry Assu speaks out forthrightly for the claims of his family and his people, as it is proper for a Kwagiulth chief to do.

He opens his autobiography with an account of the "Flood" that covered the earth at a time when the We-Wai-Kai were living at their mainland village of Tekya on Jackson Bay in Topaze Harbour, where they were saved by the great chief Wai-Kai. Coastal Indians share this origin story of the "Flood," and only the location within range of the village of the tribe and the name of the supernatural saviour ("first man") shifts from region to region. The territory settled by the survivors becomes theirs by sacred sanction, providing moral authority to title to the lands and surrounding waters.

During the period in which Harry Assu was engaged in relating the history of his people, the land claims of the Indians of British Columbia were drawn up and registered with the Office of Native Claims in Ottawa (1983). Since no comprehensive land treaty was signed with the native people in this area and they were not defeated by conquest, they claim aboriginal title to the land. This claim has not yet been acknowledged by the provincial government. Harry Assu was one of the chiefs of the Kwagiulth Nation whose expertise was sought in drawing up the boundaries of the Kwagiulth claims, particularly those areas used by the We-Wai-Kai band. All claims by coastal Indian tribes in British Columbia will encompass the land and sea areas that were within their aboriginal control. Much of the interest shown by Harry Assu in the migration and settlement of the We-Wai-Kai derives from the actual need to recall this history at a time when it was of vital importance to his people.

In this context of close scrutiny of areas controlled by neighbouring Lekwiltok bands of the Kwagiulth nation, a longstanding dispute between the We-Wai-Kum band of Campbell River and the We-Wai-Kai band of Cape Mudge erupted over the rightful ownership of the reserve on which the We-Wai-Kum are settled at the mouth of the Campbell River and of a reserve on the Quinsam River, a tributary of the Campbell on which the We-Wai-Kai of Cape Mudge are settled. As early as 1982, when our work on the manuscript was begun, Harry Assu commented on the circumstances surrounding this dispute. His testimony was sought in 1985 when the We-Wai-Kum of Campbell River sued the

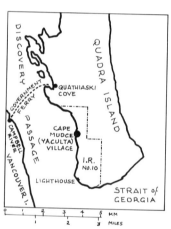

Map 1
Village of Cape Mudge, the major settlement of the We-Wai-Kai band. MacGregor/Stewart, 1985

We-Wai-Kai of Cape Mudge and the federal government over ownership of the land at Quinsam.

The large portion of the book which Harry Assu devotes to his life in
the fishing business indicates the key position which this occupation
holds in the lives of the We-Wai-Kai people, who now, as always,
depend upon the great runs of Pacific salmon for their livelihood. Harry
Assu gives us some fascinating glimpses into the original beliefs and
practices still current when he was a boy and some that prevailed in his
grandfather's time; he also provides us with his assessment of life in the
old cannery days along the coast. Since fishing is the traditional way of
life of the We-Wai-Kai of Cape Mudge, they are deeply concerned about
maintained this essential aspect of native culture in what has become a
lucrative but risky business. While fishing still provides the desired
mobility and requires the skill and willingness to risk life and gamble all
in a highly competitive game that Indians find satisfying, there is for the
first time in history no certainty that the generations to come can follow
in the traditional way of life. It is against this background of threat of loss
of Indian identity that the intensity of Harry Assu's concerns in this matter can best be understood.

Another aspect of life to which Harry Assu devotes considerable attention is the role of the church at Cape Mudge. During the preparation
of this book, feeling was aroused amongst native members of the church
over whether an apology should be made by the United Church of Canada for having suppressed native spirituality and requiring that Christianity be expressed in terms of European culture. While some led this
spirited movement, others felt that an apology was unwarranted and
that the call for one drew unfortunate attention to distinctions of race
between members of the integrated congregation. It is in this climate of
concern that Harry Assu tells us what he knows of the missionary experience at Cape Mudge.

Of all the circumstances that provide a background to the selection of
topics which Harry Assu has made, the one with the most immediate recent impact has been the return of the "Potlatch Collection" originally
seized under threat of jail sentence by federal government agencies in
1922, the building of museums to house the returned masks and other
paraphernalia, and the renewed potlatching and feasting that accompanied this signal event.

My acquaintance with the Assu family and the villagers of Cape
Mudge extends over a period of twenty years since I researched a first
ethnography of Cape Mudge. After we retired to Quadra Island a short
distance from the reserve in 1974, my husband and I met frequently

with people there and became good friends with Harry Assu. In the spring of 1982, he hosted "In Praise of Native Authors" at Cape Mudge during National Book Festival, an event that I helped to co-ordinate. It was then that he realized that a book could be the means of sharing the history of his people through the generations, for he was much concerned that the youth of the Lekwiltok villages were growing up without any knowledge of their own history or what constituted their own Indianness. Because of my long association with the people of Cape Mudge, I was as anxious as he to engage in this endeavour, and so our collaboration began.

Through the fall of 1982 and the spring of 1983 we met on a regular schedule at his home to explore his story and to tape and transcribe what he felt was important to pass on to his people. We continued these sessions from time to time at my home as the manuscript began to take form. There were breaks for Harry Assu's busy schedule and travel and for an extended period following the death of his beloved wife Ida.

In the writing I have expanded the phrases Harry Assu used in ordinary conversation to convey his thoughts into sentences that clarify meaning and permit the narrative to flow. All the written work was reviewed with him, and if he felt uncomfortable with the way his words sounded when read back by me, we worked again to suggest his intended meaning in a way satisfactory to him. Sometimes he was amused or taken aback at hearing his words coming out of my mouth, but he was always patient, never exasperated, and remained at all times an amiable and dignified gentleman. Constant revisions were made as we moved back and forth in the text correcting and enriching the material.

Harry Assu's sons and their families were invited to read the chapters as they developed, and while they made valuable suggestions for further enquiry, they did not suggest alterations in content. They said that while they did not necessarily agree with every opinion expressed, they had certainly heard their father saying the things that have been recorded here.

Assu family members from several generations met with us to confer on family genealogy and help produce the chart which defines the relationships to which Harry Assu so frequently refers. It soon becomes evident in everyday interaction with Indian people on this Coast that the individual is defined in terms of a network of family connections with such facility that for the uninitiated the lines of descent can be hard to follow. Genealogical charts of Canada's first families are urgently needed before the information fades from the memory of elders and is permanently lost to the generations to come.

Harry and I met once a week for seven weeks with other family members who had organized the potlatch of 1984 which Harry Assu describes in the last chapter of the book. Ten hours of conversation were taped and transcribed while a video of the event was played. This invaluable process provided me with a framework for the description Harry Assu has made of this great ceremonial occasion.

In addition to English, Harry Assu speaks Kwakwala, the language used by the Kwagiulth people still familiar with it. Our sessions were conducted in English, and the orthography used for native terms is that developed by Peter Wilson for liq̓ʷala, the dialect of Kwakwala used in the Lekwiltok area comprising today the villages at Cape Mudge, Campbell River, and Comox. All use of native terms was heard in context in order to accurately transcribe those sounds made in Kwakwala that do not occur in the English language.

In telling his story, Harry Assu speaks out against the oppression of the past while remaining optimistic for the future of his people, and his fellow man. In the past his hopes rested upon higher education for native people, and this struggle in his most productive years was not in vain; seven of his descendants have attended universities. He takes pride in the defiance of his people against paternalistic and authoritarian government that worked to its own agenda without regard for its impact on native people, for example, the suppression of the potlatch, which was the central organizing principle of Coastal Indian life, and the seizure by government agents of potlatch regalia. This source of anguish has only partly been mitigated by the recent repossession of these family treasures from Canada's leading museums.

Harry Assu is a big man, in his position as an elder of the Cape Mudge people, in his physical stature, and in his understanding. He looks confidently to the future. In co-authoring his autobiography, I have tried to keep his voice and the warmth for mankind and humour that resonates in it.

The thriving village of Cape Mudge attests to the buoyancy of its people. Their lives today and competitive position in the highly technical fishing industry speak well for the leaders of the people who have adroitly guided their financial and political affairs. Plans are developed for diversifying the economy and enriching the realm of traditional ceremony. Harry Assu looks back over a lifetime of struggle and accomplishment with justifiable pride. Now let us listen to his story.

Joy Inglis

To my father, Billy Assu of Cape Mudge, who guided his people through the difficult years of transition from traditional to modern life. He gave over sixty years of continuous effective leadership to his people.

1
Origins of My People

I was born in 1905 at Cape Mudge. When I was six years old, my father, Billy Assu, took me to see our old village t̓əka[1] on the Mainland in Topaze Harbour. Tekya[2] means soil. If you take up the dirt of the land in your hand that is what is meant by the name. My father told me, "That's where our people used to live."

There's a river there. That's why the village was there, right beside the river. There are two big long totem poles standing up about two hundred feet apart and fifty feet high – taller than any that were put up here at Cape Mudge. I can only remember that on one of these there was a whale with a man carved below. There is no village there today. Tekya is not on marine charts.

The mountain close behind the village is where our people were saved at the time of the Flood. It is not a big mountain, but it is the biggest mountain around there. The heavy square rock where the canoes of our people tied on when the water rose up high is still up there. There is salt water up there too.

Weqaʔi was the chief who told the people "It's going to flood." I don't know the meaning of his name. My people, the weweq̓eʔ take our name from him. We are the We-Wai-Kai band. The weweq̓əm people in Campbell River get their name from him too. They are the We-Wai-Kum band. Wai-Kai[3] is a great name. The Dick family from Cape Mudge own that name.

Wai-Kai wove cedar ropes from the anchor rock on top of the mountain down to the village and told the people when the flood comes to tie the canoes onto the rope. He warned them four years before it happened! A lot of people didn't believe him. They kept saying, "You crazy? Where's all this water going to come from?" When the seas rose

Plate 2
Wai-Kai, saviour of the We-Wai-Kai
people of Cape Mudge. Part of a
memorial pole belonging to John Dick,
Sr. No longer standing in the village of
Cape Mudge. Photographed in 1979 by
Wilma Wood

up to the tops of the mountains, the people were saved. Wai-Kai, the chief of our people, was in the lead canoe with all the rest strung out behind him. When the water went down, we lost one canoe. The canoe was named x̌aʔisala. It drifted north and landed in Kitimat. Today the tribe up there is called Haisla – same name as the canoe. The other canoes came ashore right around here in our own territory.

The people of our band, the We-Wai-Kai of Cape Mudge, are the farthest south of the canoe people cut off Wai-Kai's rope at the time of the Flood. Between these places we all speak languages that sound something the same, but for us a big break comes up north at Rivers Inlet. The Oweekeeno tribe there speak a different language. It has a tune in it. It sounds like our language, but we can't really understand what they say.

Our people speak kʷakʷala language (Kwakwala). The elders like to talk to each other in our language, but everybody can speak English now. The kids are learning our language in the schools here, and it's going pretty well. Even some of the non-Indian kids are learning to speak our language.

Everybody around here used to speak Kwakwala and in the villages of our people north to Smith Sound. These are the people we called to the big gathering that went on here at Cape Mudge. They are the people of Fort Rupert, Quatsino, Smith Inlet and Blunden Harbour, Alert Bay, Hope Island, Village Island, Gilford Island, Turnour Island, Knight Inlet, Kingcome Inlet, Harbledown Island and the Hopetown people on Watson Island, and our southern people at Salmon River and Campbell River. (Map 2)

My people, the We-Wai-Kai of Cape Mudge village, came to our village on Quadra Island about two hundred years ago.[4] We were many years coming. All the Indian people moved around a lot with the seasons at the time when we still lived in our village beside Jackson Bay. We had our fishing stations, berrying places, hunting places. We went into Knight Inlet, on the right-hand side of the river near the mouth of the X̌inaX̌ina (Klinaklini) River, for dᶻaxʷən; that's eulachon fish. We had buildings there and made oil for our people in the early spring.

We were moving around in Johnstone Strait too and came all the way down to this area around the Campbell River at certain times of year. We came for the blueback salmon off Cape Mudge in spring. We wanted this place because we could get all five species of salmon twelve months of the year. The reason our people moved from the mainland villages to the Campbell River was to secure the fishing grounds here.

After leaving Topaze Harbour we were at Whiterock Pass between

Maurelle and Read Islands for five years. (Map 3) We called that place ŧaŧapaʔulis. The names means the flood when canoes can be launched. Before it was dredged, the passage used to go dry. There is a reserve there now called Tatpoose, but it belongs to the Salish people who live at Squirrel Cove on Cortes Island.

Later we moved to Drew Harbour, which we call caɫcəx̌isa. That's a big bay sheltered from the southeast storms on the east side of Quadra Island. Chum and coho salmon used to run in the stream there. After that we moved across the island to the west side of Gowlland Harbour to ǧʷiǧʷakulis village.

After staying two or three years at Gowlland Harbour on Quadra Island, we moved across Discovery Passage to the mouth of the Campbell

Map 2
The coast of British Columbia and adjacent territories with inset of the central coast showing the extent of the land and sea claims of the native people as outlined by the Kwakiutl District Council and the ten village settlements of the bands in 1984. Hilary Stewart, 1988

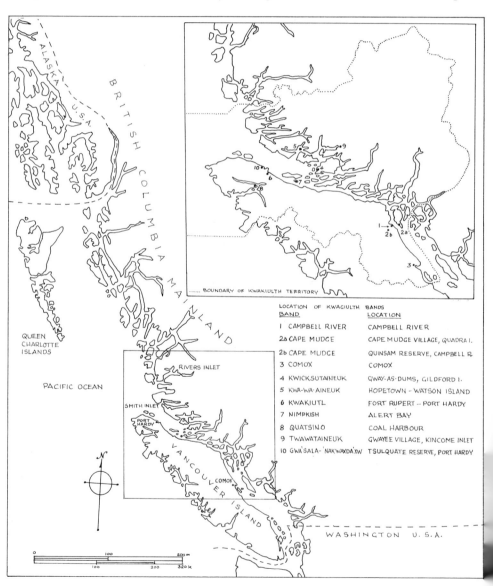

LOCATION OF KWAGIULTH BANDS

BAND	LOCATION
1 CAMPBELL RIVER	CAMPBELL RIVER
2a CAPE MUDGE	CAPE MUDGE VILLAGE, QUADRA I.
2b CAPE MUDGE	QUINSAM RESERVE, CAMPBELL R.
3 COMOX	COMOX
4 KWICKSUTAINEUK	QWAY-AS-DUMS, GILDFORD I.
5 KWA-WA-AINEUK	HOPETOWN – WATSON ISLAND
6 KWAKIUTL	FORT RUPERT – PORT HARDY
7 NIMPKISH	ALERT BAY
8 QUATSINO	COAL HARBOUR
9 TWAWATAINEUK	GWAYEE VILLAGE, KINCOME INLET
10 GWA'SALA-'NAKWAXDA'XW	TSULQUATE RESERVE, PORT HARDY

River and settled on the spit for five years. (see insert on Map 3) This estuary area was called ƛamatəxʷ. There was no white settlement on the Campbell River then, and we were the only native people wintering there at that time. From the spit location we moved upriver a short ways. The area from the south side of the mouth of the river up to around Lane Field, in present-day Campbellton, we called ʔaƛigalis. My own family had a house on the river there.

Finally the We-Wai-Kai moved to our present village site at Cape Mudge near the southern tip of Quadra Island, where our people have lived ever since. But when I was a boy my family returned every fall to our place on the Campbell River where the family big house had once stood, and we caught and smoked the fall run of salmon. We had always

Map 3
Migration route of the We-Wai-Kai band from Tekya on the Mainland of British Columbia to their present villages of Cape Mudge on Quadra Island and Quinsam on Vancouver Island. MacGregor/Stewart, 1985

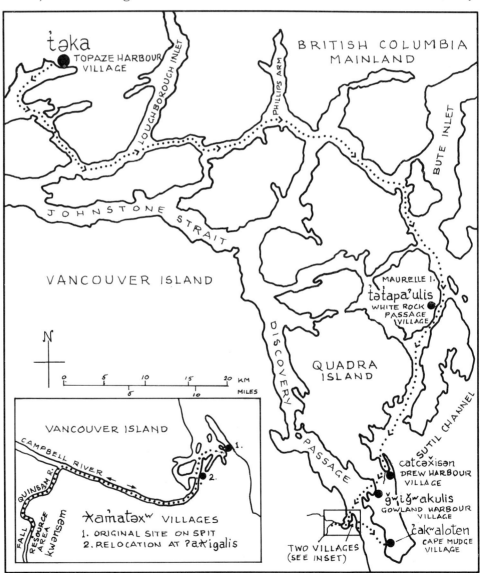

done that ever since the We-Wai-Kai had our village on the Campbell River and even after commercial fishing started.

My wife Ida's people, the Dicks, had smokehouses there too. All our people went there every fall. Our place for smoking fish on the Campbell River was on the south side, nearly opposite the big island in the river we called łədis.

When our people were living at x̣aṁatəxʷ, they used to go in summer up to kʷʼənsəm river area for deer-hunting, berry-picking, and trapping fish in the Quinsam River. It used to be a big grassy meadow. Our men went further inland too and hunted along the Campbell and Buttle Lakes.

Quinsam prairie where our people stayed was made a reserve of the We-Wai-Kai band. As I see it, both sides of the river bank are reserve land, though the maps don't show it. The We-Wai-Kai own five reserves in all, and almost everywhere else the river is inside the reserve to make sure that we're the ones to use it.

I have heard that long, long ago, before our people ever came to Jackson Bay and to this Strait of Georgia region, we were up around Queen Charlotte Strait moving around with the Village Island and Turnour Island people and all the others there. That's where most of our

Map 4
Migration route of the Lekwiltok tribe of the Kwagiulth Nation from the Cape Scott area on Vancouver Island to the northern Strait of Georgia region. MacGregor/Stewart, 1985

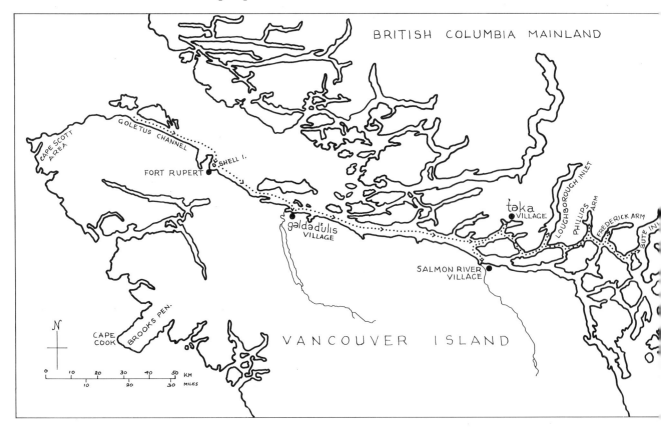

Kwakwala-speaking people live now, though many were once over on the west coast of Vancouver Island north on Brooks Peninsula and farther north.

Henry Hunt of Fort Rupert said that our people settled at Cape Mudge stopped at Shell Island about one-quarter mile from his village when they were coming south from Cape Scott.[5] (Map 4).

There is a story that goes with the carved pole that stood in front of my father's big house at Cape Mudge that tells about our people when they lived farther north.

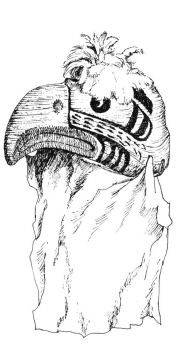

*Figure 1
Kuloose mask of Billy Assu, carved by Mungo Martin (979.1.57 KM). Drawing by Hilary Stewart, 1985*

> The Kuloose came to earth as a bird and was transformed into a man who was called Hakuweela. This man wandered about for a long time seeking a mate and finally found a woman belonging to what is now known as the Wewayakay or Cape Mudge Band. He found her at the extreme northern end of Vancouver Island at a place called Cukwakileese. They married and had children. Hakuweela was warned in a dream to be on his guard always at low tide. Every night, when the tide was low, he would go out and watch. One night he saw something which seemed to be on fire. When he saw this he ran into the house but heard lots of noise outside. When he went out the noise stopped, but a log, which seemed to be on fire, was standing outside his house. Looking out to sea he was surprised to see a canoe full of people. Seeing that they had brought him fire he thanked them. They told him that there was a nest in the top of a tree which he could use as a refuge as some people were coming to make war on him. Then to his surprise the canoe turned into a whale, noted on the totem, and swam away.
>
> Not long after a war party attacked him knowing he had lots of food. When Hakuweela and his family saw the enemy coming they climbed to the tree nest, using a ladder made of cedar bark. They carried huge stones with them. When the enemy attacked they threw the stones down on them and eventually conquered them. After this, when he was in doubt, he would have a dream in which the tree would tell him what to do.

This pole was given to the Quocksister family at Campbell River in 1915 when my sister Susan married Johnny Quocksister. It was sold from over there. When it was returned to the Kwagiulth Museum at Cape Mudge from Calgary in the spring of 1984, that story was in with the papers that came with it.

The bird on my father's pole is an eagle, not qulus (Kuloose). Whale is

Figure 2
The Billy Assu Memorial Pole at the Kwagiulth Museum. Drawing from an early photograph by Hilary Stewart,

one of our most important family crests. We have the right to dance the qulus mask; my father's qulus mask is in the Kwagiulth Museum at Cape Mudge, but it's not on our family poles as far as I know.

Up north we had a village long ago name gəldəd⁼ulis; that means big long beach. It was on a stretch of beach to the south of the Nimpkish River on Vancouver Island. Nearby upriver was a village of the ṅəmǧis (Nimpkish) tribe who later moved from there over to Alert Bay on Cormorant Island.[6]

Our old people remembered what happened when the We-Wai-Kai were living at gəldəd⁼ulis. There was this box full of coppers which our people got in a marriage exchange with the Turnour Island tribe. It was lifted from us by trickery, and there was fighting and a lot of people were killed when our people went up the river to bring back the box. I don't know, but it could be the reason why our We-Wai-Kai band began moving south from there into the Strait of Georgia. Our villages were along the Mainland from Port Neville to Bute Inlet and on Vancouver Island from the Salmon River at Kelsey Bay to Comox in the south. There were thousands of our people moving south over time, and we mostly potlatched amongst ourselves in the neighbouring villages of our liǧʷiłda?x̌ʷ (Lekwiltok) tribe.[7]

Potlatch is a Chinook jargon word. Everybody spoke this trade language when I was young. We call these big potlatches ṗəsa in our language, but now it's called potlatch by Indians and everybody else all up and down the coast. One of my father's names was ṗəsala, meaning Potlatcher. Important families call the people to a potlatch. Then we tell our family history and show our dances and give away names that go with the dances. We give away money and goods to everybody who's invited, and that's what the word potlatch means: "giving away."

After 1900, when we got gas boats and money was coming in from fishing and logging, we called all the fourteen tribes of our Kwagiulth people to Cape Mudge for potlatches more often. High-ranking men here called the West Coast tribes on Vancouver Island and sometime the Salish tribes as far south as Squamish on the Mainland and Saanich around Victoria.

When the Lekwiltok moved south into this part of the country where we are now, there was a Salish people here we called ǵumuks (Comox). Tekya at Topaze Harbour was the first village of the We-Wai-Kai band in the Strait. Our next village was at Salmon River on Vancouver Island. At Salmon River village the Salish people stayed on and joined with the Lekwiltok. They trusted each other, married, and worked together. Ever since it has been like that. By the time th reserves were laid out (1880's), Salmon River was No. 1 reserve of the Lekwiltok.

The Comox were moving south (Map 5) at that time from their villages along Johnstone Strait and Discovery Passage, and they settled in Courtenay Bay near where the reserve is now at Comox.[8] Some of the families at Salmon River village moved down to Comox at that time, and more went down later to join their families when the population was way down, and there were only a few people left in the Salmon River village. The two bands amalgamated in the 1940's, and no one is left in the old village of the Walitsum band on the Salmon River. When the bands amalgamated, they came under the agent at Alert Bay. Now Comox is the southernmost village of the Lekwiltok tribe.[9]

Map 5
Southern movement of the Lekwiltok tribe and their Vancouver Island-Comox-speaking allies.
MacGregor/Stewart, 1985

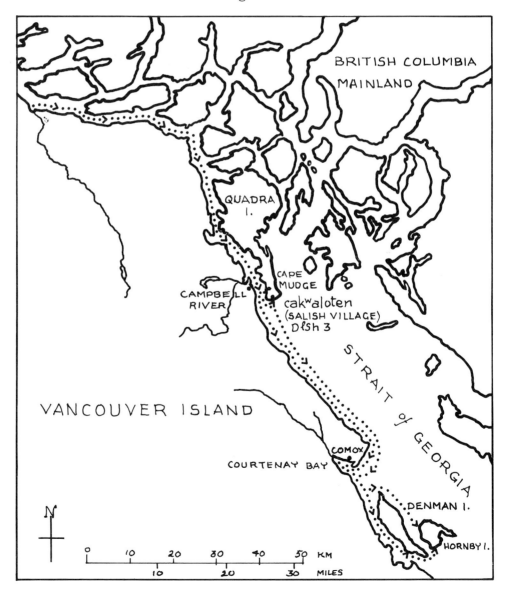

At the time we first established our village of Cape Mudge, the Comox-speaking people still had their big village about two miles south on the high sandy cliffs at the tip of Quadra Island. The village was called ćakʷalotən. We took that name (Tsquloten) for our village here.[10] Those people in the big village on the cliffs eventually went down to Comox village in Courtenay Bay to join with their relatives there.

Our We-Wai-Kai people here at Cape Mudge village began going down to Comox in spring. We kept our winter village here. Our Lek wiltok people had a village beside the Comox in Courtenay Bay. That whole area, including Denman and Hornby Islands, was a great place for herring and wild bulbs in the spring and berries in the summer. Shellfish were taken on Tree Island and cedars for canoes on Hornby Island, and deer were trapped on Denman Island. We shared that place together.[1]

Mary Clifton of Comox (née Frank), who is the mother of Cissy Assu, my son Steve's wife, is the last of the Island-Comox speakers. Mary is now over ninety years old. She speaks and understands the Comox and Kwakwala languages and English.

Mary Clifton's sister Maggie lived here at Cape Mudge. She was the wife of Johnny Dick. Their son Ivan married my daughter Pearl. Mary and Maggie had a grandmother of the Kwiksutaineuk tribe of Gilford Is

Figure 3
Harry Assu Family Tree. The descendants of Ida and Harry Assu can be found in Appendix 9.

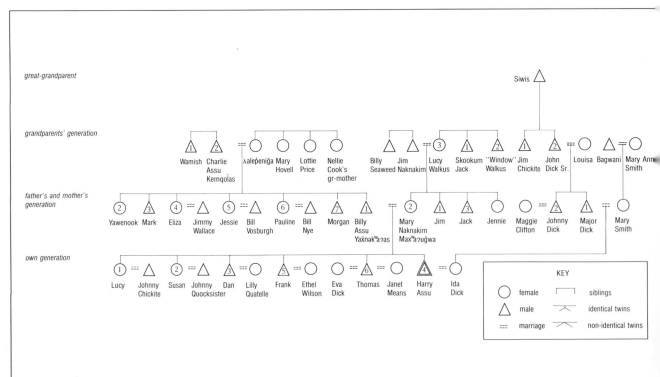

land who married into the Comox band. Intermarriage has been going on for many years. My own grandfather, Charley Assu, had a sister-in-law, Nellie Cook's mother, who married a man from the Comox people who settled here at Cape Mudge. His name was George Hamilton.

We have a good feeling for all those tribes down Vancouver Island to around Cowichan. My grandfather told me that the way we overcame hard feelings between neighbouring groups of people was through making good marriages with them. In the case of the Nanaimo, our people working in the mines at Union Bay in my father's time got to know them, and we have had close feelings for those people ever since. Tom Price, a member of the Kwaikah band of our tribe from the Phillips Arm area on the Mainland, moved here to Cape Mudge, and Price families still live here. He had an uncle named Ray Seaweed in Nanaimo, and that man has phoned me every Christmas for twenty-one years!

The Salish people from Cowichan, Ladysmith, and Chemainus and Nanaimo people used to camp in our reserve here for the summer every year of my life until the 1960's. They camped on a bench of land north of the lighthouse within sight of our village. They fished from there and sold their salmon to the cannery at Quathiaski Cove in the early days. Families came, and some of the women spent the summer spinning wool

Plate 3
"View of an Indian Village on Pt Mudge, Gulf of Georgia." Drawing by William Sykes, midshipman on H.M.S. Discovery, Captain George Vancouver, 1792. The village shown is Tsquloten, an important village of the Vancouver Island-Comox. Reproduced by permission of the Hydrographer of the Navy

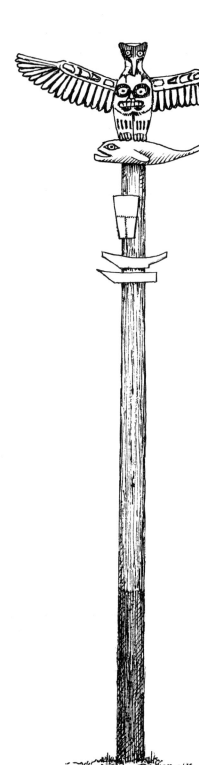

Figure 4
Jim Smith Memorial Pole once standing at Cape Mudge. Drawing from an early photograph by Hilary Stewart, 1985

and knitting Cowichan sweaters. We have been friends with them for a long time. And that includes the people as far south as Cowichan on Vancouver Island and the Salish on the Mainland as far south as North Vancouver.

We have good relations with the mainland Salish people at Church House and Squirrel Cove and with the Sliammon at Powell River as well. We call the Powell River people ɬaʔamin. But we were never as close to the Salish on the Mainland as a whole people as we were with the Island-Comox. The Salish nearest us in the Northern Strait of Georgia on the Mainland used to live in the Interior beyond the inlets, so I don't think our people saw much of them in the old days before the white men came. They seemed to have been more broad-shouldered and not so tall as most of our people – a different people.

Jim Smith, brother of Mary Anne Smith, who was my wife's grandmother, had a medium-size old-style house here at Cape Mudge. He was a Kwaikah from Phillips Arm. He had family in the Sliammon village at Powell River. They are mainland Salish. My grandmother, Lucy Naknakim (née Walkus), was Kwaikah. Tom Price was related to the Alex Paul family in Church House on the Mainland. The Church House people are from the tribe who once lived way up beyond the end of Bute Inlet.[12]

Another connection with the mainland Salish in my family came about in this way. My sister Lucy was married to Johnny Chickite. The Chickites are We-Wai-Kai.[13] "Chickite" means to throw away. It is a potlatch name meaning he is so rich he can just throw away his wealth at the potlatch. The sons of my sister Lucy and Johnny Chickite (Art and Edward) married Annie and Nellie Seville, sisters from Squirrel Cove, and brought them here to Cape Mudge where they became members of our band. The people of Squirrel Cove are the Klahuse tribe, a mainland Salish group who once lived far up beyond the head of Toba Inlet. There are a lot of Chickite families in the village. Allen Chickite, son of Edward and Annie, has served as elected chief councillor of the Cape Mudge Band.

As far as I know the fights and raids and taking captives was all over with one hundred and forty years ago. The worst raids were with the Indians at the southern end of Vancouver Island around Victoria. We know that. We also know that the Haida and the people all down the coast were afraid of the Cape Mudge! Our warriors were rough. Everybody kept out of their way! The real leaders of our people were the chiefs.

People used to be afraid of passing by our village in their canoes for fear of being taken captive. None of those families are left in the villages around here. The last died out during the 1918 flu epidemic.

We once had a fight with the Fort Ruperts, a part of the Kwagiulth people. They came down here in force to attack our village of Cape Mudge. This was done so the head guys in the war canoes could get fame for the war party. Every village was looking out for itself in those days. At the time we had guns in our fort, but we did not fire right on the Fort Rupert people. They put in with their canoes on the beach north of the village. Then they came on, hiding behind their canoes, which they pushed along from the edge of the beach. There was a lot of firing and threats, but I think it was mostly to clear the air after some quarrel. The leader of their people put his hands apart to show that it was a useless business. And the whole thing ended. They really came so they could settle. No more war!

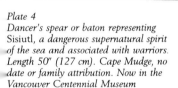

Plate 4
Dancer's spear or baton representing Sisiutl, *a dangerous supernatural spirit of the sea and associated with warriors. Length 50' (127 cm). Cape Mudge, no date or family attribution. Now in the Vancouver Centennial Museum (A1890)*

2
Organization of My People

Nowadays our people here use the term Kwagiulth for all the Kwakwala-speaking tribes north to Smith Inlet. Beyond there the Heiltsuk language begins. Almost all our southern tribes are represented by the Kwakiutl District Council.[1] The name Kwagiulth (or Kwakiutl) has been spelled in all sorts of ways by missionaries, government agents, and anthropologists. It's the name of the tribe at Fort Rupert near Port Hardy on Vancouver Island, but we all use that name.[2]

Each tribe of the Kwagiulth Nation has its own name. It is hard to write the name of our tribe, which is liǧʷiɫdaʔx̌ʷ (Lekwiltok). It is spelled Yaculta on marine charts.

So far as I know the Lekwiltok tribe was made up of four bands. We were always together in the potlatch. When I was a boy, all the bands of the Lekwiltok came together here at Cape Mudge for the potlatch and winter dancing. We were the centre for that.[3]

In those early days the four bands of the Lekwiltok were the We-Wai-Kai of Cape Mudge, the Walitsum of Salmon River, near Kelsey Bay, the We-Wai-Kum of Campbell River, and the Kwaikah of Campbell River.[4] The Walitsum don't live at Salmon River any more. They amalgamated with the Comox. Our people, the We-Wai-Kai, lived here at Cape Mudge.

The We-Wai-Kum of Campbell River were from mainland villages on Loughborough Inlet, Heydon Bay, and Greene Point Rapids (Map 6). The Kwaikah joined the We-Wai-Kum at Campbell River from their villages on the Mainland around Phillips Arm. The name Kwaikah means to club. They were warriors.

Our people, the We-Wai-Kai of Cape Mudge, were the first of the Lekwiltok bands on the Mainland to move into the territory on Discovery Passage between Vancouver Island and Quadra Island where we are now. We were gone from our winter village near Jackson Bay when they surveyed for Indian reserves in our Lekwiltok territory. So although Tekya in Jackson Bay is very important to our people, we don't have a reserve there.

The We-Wai-Kum and Kwaikah Bands moved their people down from the Mainland to Campbell River more slowly. Many of the We-Wai-Kum and Kwaikah were still in their mainland villages at the time they made up the reserves in the 1880's. That is why they were able to get reserve land over there. A few were still there in the 1920's, but everyone else had moved down to the reserve on the spit at the Campbell River by then. They went back and forth to the Mainland for hunt-

Map 6
Movements of the Lekwiltok tribes from their village on the Mainland of British Columbia to their present locations on the east coast of Vancouver Island

ing and logging. Around 1920 the We-Wai-Kum moved off the Camp-bell River spit so they could sell that land. They still live on land next to the spit, and that is their one village today.

Twelve reserves were set aside for the Lekwiltok tribe. Indian Reserve No. 1 was the reserve of the Walitsum of Salmon River. The next five reserves (I.R. 2, 3, 4, 5, and 6) belong to the We-Wai-Kum and Kwaikah at their old village sites on the Mainland. They also own I.R. 11 on the Campbell River where they live now.

Our band, the We-Wai-Kai, owns four reserves on Quadra Island (formerly Valdez). They are I.R. 7, 8, 9, and 10. Number 10, Cape Mudge, is our village. Also we own I.R. 12 at Quinsam, a river flowing into the Campbell River on Vancouver Island. Both Cape Mudge and Quinsam are settled by our people though fewer families live at Quinsam. Both are run by the We-Wai-Kai band.

A head man of the Loughborough people, We-Kai-Kum band, was still alive when I was seventeen years old in 1922. We went up there fishing. He was an important man, and that was his territory. We called him Loughborough Bill. We went to this Heydon Bay, and McPherson, my skipper, told me that there's this ba-aad Indian up there at Phillips Arm and Loughborough Inlet, and he's going to try to stop us so we can't go in and fish. Loughborough Bill didn't like people coming in there to fish in the place he owned, and he chased boats out. Oh, there were a lot of fish in there! And my skipper wanted to take them. So he said to me, "We're going in! You talk to him in your language." So we started in. Loughborough Bill shot out at us in a big canoe.

"Who are you?" he yelled.

"From Cape Mudge," I shouted.

"Who is your father?"

I hollered "yax̌nək̓ʷaʔas".

"Oh!... I see.... You can come in!"

It has always made me laugh to think about it. I guess it was the first time I realized that my father's name opened doors.

All the reserves we have today were places we used for villages or fish-ing stations or places we went for food at the time they were surveyed in the 1880's. But, of course, we owned everything here and still hold title to this land and its waters and are claiming for it now.

When I was around eleven years old, my father started going down to Victoria with other chiefs on the coast to let the government know that we own these lands and water. My father was told, "The interior Indians get big reserves because they need the land for ranching and trapping, but you got small reserves because you need the water for fishing."

Map 7
"Plan of the Laich-Kwil-Tach Indian
Reserves." Original drawings in
watercolour on linen, dated 18 May
1889 by E. M. Skinner and approved
by F. G. Vernon, chief commissioner of
lands and works and signed by Peter
O'Reilly, Indian reserve commissioner.
Photographed by Mila Cotic. MOA.
Courtesy Kwakiutl Museum

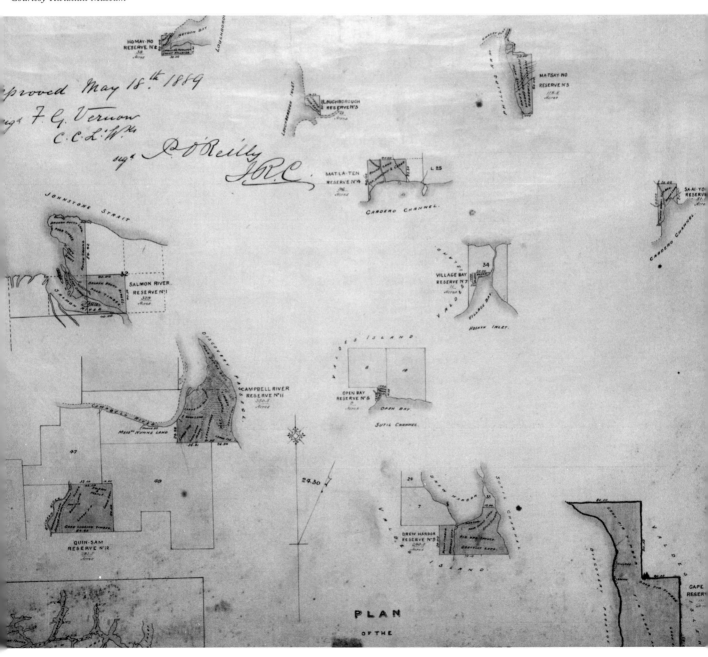

We should have a reserve at Topaze Harbour; that's where our We-Wai-Kai village was before we moved south into Discovery Passage. All our Lekwiltok people were settled from that place, after the Flood. The four bands of the Lekwiltok made our village at Tekya their place for potlatch and winter dancing in those early years of our history.[5]

Our people owned river-bank land in Knight's Inlet for eulachon fishing. This land should be made a reserve of the We-Wai-Kai.[6]

We should have our old village site at Whiterock Pass on Maurelle Island as a reserve. This place is a reserve today, but it has been transferred around and finally given to the Klahuse band. They may have spent some time in summers there in the old days, but the We-Wai-Kai were the last to settle their people there in a winter village which we occupied for about five years.

Over my lifetime there has been a dispute with the Campbell River band over the ownership of the Campbell River estuary. Our people settled there before the We-Wai-Kum and Kwaikah moved down here from their mainland villages. By that time we were living in our village here at Cape Mudge where we could get all five species of salmon all year round; but in the fall we always moved back to our fishing stations on the Campbell River to take the chum salmon for the winter.

I think the trouble over ownership of the land at Campbell River is because the government got confused by the names being so alike: We-Wai-Kai and We-Wai-Kum. In the 1930's a meeting was called here at Cape Mudge to try to come to a settlement. It was a big showdown. Johnny Quocksister, who was chief over there in Campbell River at the time, wanted amalgamation of the two bands. He was married to my sister, and as my father was chief here at Cape Mudge, it could have been a good way to solve the problem of ownership. But other chiefs at Campbell River got angry and opposed amalgamation, so my father said, "No! Leave it the way it is." We couldn't understand that. My brothers and I were for amalgamation. It was only later on we figured that my father wanted good relations between the people more than he wanted settlement of the question of land.

Our We-Wai-Kai people are married with the We-Wai-Kum of Campbell River, and it makes it very hard on everybody to carry on these bitter disputes. During that struggle in the thirties, my father spoke for Cape Mudge, and Bill Roberts and Jim Smith from Campbell River opposed him. My father and Bill Roberts were close "cousins," through Wamish, the greatest chief at Cape Mudge in those early times. Wamish was my father's uncle. (Father's father kəmqoĺas was brother to Wamish.) Bill Roberts' mother was Wamish's only daughter. She mar-

Plate 5
Signing the Position Statement on Land and Sea Claims. Basil Ambers, Chairman of the Kwakiutl District Council, standing in the back, and Bob Joseph, signing the document which was approved and signed by chiefs of all eleven tribes of the Kwagiulth Nation on 22 May 1984. Photo by John Gordon, courtesy of the Campbell River Courier

ried George Quocksister from Campbell River. (Bill gave up the name Quocksister when he joined the army and they couldn't say his name; so they called him "Roberts.") My own daughter Jean is married to Bill Roberts' son Tony. He is chief councillor of the Campbell River band. When she married Tony I told her not to worry; there wasn't going to be any more fighting over who owns the reserves.

Well, that's not what has happened. Some people at Campbell River still say that our reserve at Quinsam should be theirs. Quinsam belonged to the families of my father and my mother: Assu and Naknakim. It was my grandfather, Jim Naknakim, who took Mr. Green to the Campbell River and Quinsam when he was surveying for the reserves in the 1880's.[7] If it wasn't for my grandfather, Green would never have got in to Quinsam. There was no trail then, and Green tried to turn back three times, but my grandfather urged him on. Our people always went there from our village on the Campbell River by loading our canoes and heading up the Campbell to the Quinsam River in late summer and fall. Later, in 1917, it was my father, my brother Dan and myself, and others of our family who built the first road into Quinsam and built a small house there for hunting. We planted fruit trees there and dug a large garden for potatoes.

When Quinsam was my grandfather Jim Naknakim's hunting grounds, he built a platform there in a big tree; the stump is still there. Deer skins were selling to traders for one dollar each, and he could get a hundred in a day. Deer were just feeding around there like sheep.

Fred Dick of Cape Mudge was the first to settle at Quinsam in modern times, and he built a family house on our reserve there. Now there are a lot of families living there. Before that we had leased Quinsam for a tree nursery and had intended to keep Quinsam for commercial use.

All our We-Wai-Kai reserves, except Quinsam, are on Quadra Island. They are at Village Bay, No. 7; Open Bay, No. 8; Drew Harbour, No. 9; and Cape Mudge, No. 10. We have a public campsite at Drew Harbour with over a hundred fully serviced units.

Village Bay and Open Bay were both in use when I was a boy, but they are not used for fishing now. We had smokehouses there and went for fall fishing. I went to Open Bay with my family. About a quarter of a mile up from the sea on the river, there were dog salmon in the pools, and we used a cork net to catch them. We just bagged them up in the net and brought them down to the smokehouses near the beach. We hard-smoked them for winter.

Today families here at Cape Mudge smoke sockeye and chum in our smokehouses for each family. Not so much is made as when I was a boy. The women can sockeye the way it was done when there was a cannery in Quathiaski Cove. We deep-freeze chums.

The food we call k̓awas requires a very special way of slicing and smoking that takes a lot of work and skill. If you want to keep k̓awas through the winter, the dog salmon (chum) is best for that. It is thinly flaked from the flesh near the bone, then smoke-dried. Quite a few of our people still make some. It is served to guests, and in the family the children especially eat it up like potato chips. Because it is special, we serve it with bread and wine for Holy Communion in the United Church here on the reserve. We used to flake halibut too, but that isn't done here anymore. m̓əlm̓adᶻu is the name that we called smoked flaked halibut.

Plate 6
Cape Mudge village, situated on the western shore of Quadra Island, across Discovery Passage from Campbell River on Vancouver Island. Roads pattern the village with the "U" forms and ovoids characteristic of Northwest Coast art. Photo by John Gordon, 1984

If we want to eat the salmon right away, we roast it on tongs over an open fire right here on the reserve. Everybody likes salmon barbecue. At our last salmon barbecue we roasted sixty-five fish to raise money for the church. We do it for the public every year. About five hundred people come to our annual barbecues. We also roast fish for events at the Museum and for our potlatches.

Every year the eulachon are brought down from Knight Inlet to Cape Mudge and Campbell River people. It's a kind of smelt. It is our custom to distribute it to our various families. It is not sold. The oil is costly where it is sold because it is scarce and people want it.

The Kwaikah band of the Lekwiltok must have been the highest in rank in the early days. They numbered around two thousand when they first moved into Georgia Strait and settled around Phillips Arm. The Comox, too, were very big at the time when they started moving into Courtenay Bay. Those two bands were the worst hit when the epidemics struck this coast. According to my grandfather and his friends, the people were dying by the hundreds on the Comox spit at the time of the flu epidemic in 1918.

We were not so bad off here and at Campbell River. In earlier times the number of our people here at Cape Mudge went down from around

Figure 5
Key to the photograph of Cape Mudge by Hilary Stewart, 1985

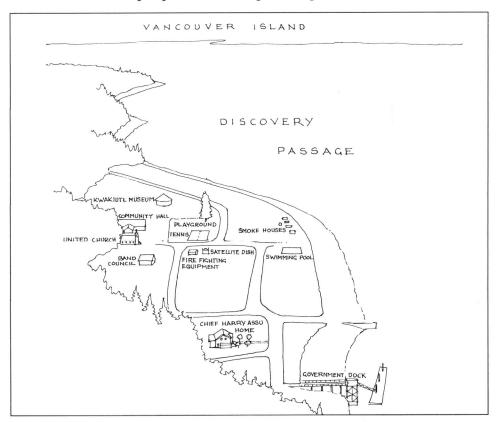

nine hundred to three hundred from smallpox epidemics. After the flu of 1918, there were only ninety-six left at Cape Mudge. These diseases were terrible everywhere. The Haida at Queen Charlotte Islands lost heavily too.[8]

The Kwagiulth people (or Southern Kwagiulth) are increasing in numbers. We are over four thousand now. The We-Wai-Kai band is the second largest of all the bands. The largest is at Alert Bay. Because there are so many families having children, the population has been growing fast. Many of our young men have married non-Indians, and they are building homes at Cape Mudge and Quinsam. I have no problem about that. I never have.

The Cape Mudge band is the biggest of the four bands of the Lekwiltok. The Campbell River are next and then the Comox. The Kwaikah are down in numbers to one family living with the Campbell River band.

There were a lot more Indians around here who lost their status and were not counted as Indians. They are Indians, but until Bill C-31 came in in 1985, they were not counted on the government list. Some men lost their status when they went to live off-reserve (enfranchise), and Indian women lost their status when they married white men. So a lot of these people have applied to come back, and the numbers in our band have shot up. Before the government changed the law, there were about four hundred in our band. Now there are over six hundred, and people are still applying. There are over one thousand in the four bands of the Lekwiltok.[9]

Most bands of our Kwakwala-speaking people have all or most of their members living off reserve. Cape Mudge is one of only three Southern Kwakiutl bands where two-thirds or more live on reserve. Everything needed for our people is right here. In Cape Mudge village we have modern homes, a community hall, nursery school, church, museum, adventure playground, swimming pool, and tennis court. We have a 150-foot tower to bring in T.V. and a satellite dish. The village has paved roads, sidewalks, a sewage system, and fire equipment. We have plans for a fishing resort on our land with marina and golf course. We have a new band office; and we are clearing the land for new homes on the ridge above the village. We have worked hard for our village.

The town of Campbell River is nearby for extra education, with stores, theatre, and so on. Our people on the Quinsam reserve live in modern homes close in to town in Campbell River.

3
Our Local Waters:
Discovery Passage and Johnstone
Strait in My Childhood and Youth

When I was about six years old, we used to go trolling every summer in canoes from our village at Cape Mudge to Duncan Bay in Discovery Passage. Our Lekwiltok people were camped all up and down Discovery Passage and Johnstone Strait in summer.

Lots of times the northwest wind would come up suddenly, and our old people would say, "That's to protect the sockeye salmon." It was dangerous to set out in canoes in a northwest wind going north from Cape Mudge into Discovery Passage for fishing.

My grandfather Jim Naknakim had power from the beings that were in the waters here in his time, especially the whales. If the canoes were having a hard time, making their way up Discovery Passage and into Johnstone Strait against the northwest wind and whales were sighted, my grandfather would holler out to them to bring a southeaster. The whales would answer by splashing their tails. The wind would then die down and soon the southeast wind would begin to blow, sending the canoes forward.

What I know of the power of eagles, raven, whales, and other Beings, I learned mostly from my mother's father, Jim Naknakim. He took us grandchildren into his house and taught us. My father's father, Charley Assu, was more of a practical man. When I was a young boy, I spent a lot of time with my grandfather Jim Naknakim. He told me the stories of his lifetime on these waters. I learned many things from him that once happened to our people, but not any more.

There was a nice beach up at Duncan Bay where the pulp mill is now.

A creek ran into the Pass there, and thirty to forty of our people from all the bands would be camped at the mouth of the stream. We called Duncan Bay gʷağəmlis, meaning bay facing north.

More people were camped up at pəlpaqȯlis. That just means in the middle. It is called Middle Point now. There was a horse camp near there where logs were skidded down to the water. Non-Indian people ran that outfit. They pulled the logs down greased skids with eight horses.

I went with my grandfather, Jim Naknakim, to Dogfish Bay on Quadra Island where a man was rendering oil from dogfish for the horse camp. Our name for Dogfish Bay is x̌ʷax̌ʷəlǧʷaʔas, and that just means place of the dogfish. You can easily get dogfish with herring bait from a

Plate 7
Harry Assu's maternal grandparents, Jim and Lucy Naknakim (née Walkus), c. 1900. Photograph in the Kwagiulth Museum

canoe early in the morning when they are on the surface feeding. Grand-father went ashore to where a white man had set up this boiler that looked like a donkey-engine. The man was buying the fish and putting up the oil in four-gallon cans to sell to the horse camp.

North of Middle Point and just before Race Point was the place where we would often start trolling back home. Lots of coho were moving south to the Campbell River – coho and pinks. In those days, if you went on up north to Salmon River (Kelsey Bay), you would see a stream of salmon under your boat fifteen to twenty feet wide, moving along south. Oh, the fish used to run up all those little creeks! No more. Very few get up since they logged.

At Menzies Bay, which we call ʔuł, that means Big Bay, there would

Plate 8
Seated at right is Charley Assu, father of Billy Assu and grandfather of Harry Assu. At the left is his youngest son, Morgan. Seated next is eldest daughter Jennie Vosburgh, holding her daughter, Margaret. The child in the centre is Nellie Cook. Standing behind her is her Aunt Tessie, daughter of Charley Assu's sister-in-law. At the right behind her father is Pauline Nye. Photograph from Joyce Halderson, courtesy of David Stouck

be three to four hundred people camped on each side of Mohun Creek. That was a big summer camp, and our people came from all over for the fishing. Oh, there used to be a lot of fish there – pinks and coho going up the streams. And it was a great place for berries in the summer.

When I was around twelve years old, I saw two or three carved poles standing in the graveyard on the south side of Mohun Creek in Menzies Bay. It was our custom in those early days to put the body in a box with big cedar planks for a lid. There was painting on the top to show the family history. There were once gravehouses at the south end of the village at Cape Mudge before the graveyard was laid out, but that was before my time. Further around the Bay from that burial place at Mohun Creek was Lamb's railroad camp on Menzies Creek.

Map 8
Campbell River to Salmon River.
MacGregor/Stewart, 1985

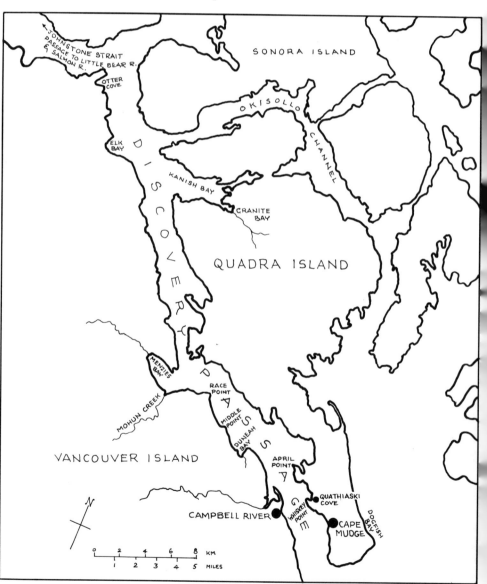

We went up into Johnstone Strait to take salmon from the fish weir built in the mouth of Little Bear River north of Rock Bay. That was the only weir still in use by the old people when I was a boy. There was a ladder leaning from shore out to a high platform over the box trap and fences below. They just floated over the trap on slack tide and rolled thirty-five to forty salmon into the boat. Two thousand sockeye, coho, and pinks were taken in the trap to feed all the people of the four bands of the Lekwiltok at one feast. Wallace, a big man in our village at Cape Mudge when I was a boy, probably owned it and let others use it. He raised a ladder and platform just like it outside his big house in the village. I saw his son David dance Hamaća on the platform when I was a boy. This dance is the most important dance of our people.

ap 9
nish Bay on Quadra Island to
tlenach Island. MacGregor/Stewart,
85

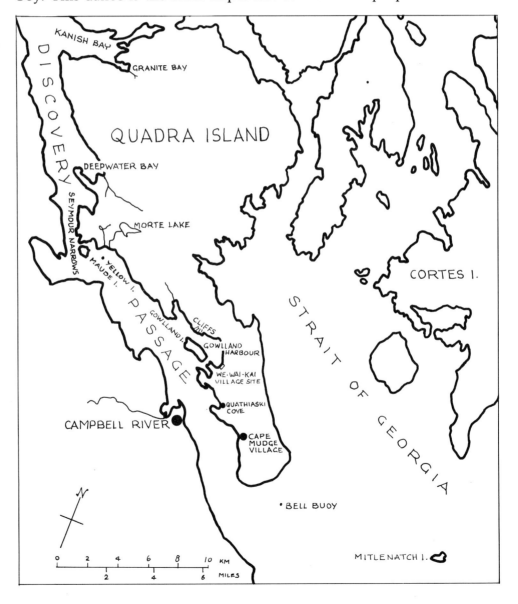

Further north in Johnstone Strait we took halibut at Salmon River in May with just a hand line. I've seen our people take sixty halibut on the first day. The biggest might weigh as much as two hundred and sixty pounds.

Things were very different around these waters in the early days of my grandfather. Many of our people were up at the Hastings Mill logging camp at qaṅis, now called Kanish Bay on Quadra Island. It was our place to go for herring in spring and berries in the fall. An owl gave warning that someone had died in our village here at Cape Mudge. All our people up there caught the tide and returned home. Sure enough, an important man was dead.

As well as dəxdəxəliɬ (Owl), ǧʷawino (Raven) was understood by some people. There was a woman here, Mrs. Oscar Lewis's mother (née Wilson), who could understand the voice of Raven. That was James Wilson's mother. James was We-Wai-Kai and my best friend when I was growing up. He died a few years ago at Comox. So, it was a long time ago when we were just kids. If something was wrong somewhere, this woman could understand the voices of Raven and tell the people where they should go to find out what had happened. With these warnings the people could get a headstart in the canoes and reach their villages in time to help out.

They made very good time racing the canoes in those days. My grandfather told me how it was done. Two strokes of the paddle were hard and deep; the third stroke was just a fanning for a rest. Twenty-two men paddled a war canoe. They made good speed.

Our Lekwiltok canoes were once down at Gooseberry Point near Bellingham. Our men were with the Lummi Indian people when word came to our village here at Cape Mudge that the Haida enemy was coming down on our village from up north.

The men left Gooseberry Point in war canoes when the sun was just setting. They arrived at our village just as dawn was breaking. It was July. That was about one hundred and thirty miles on the water in eight hours. They were in time to defend the village.

So far as I know, we have always had good relations with the Lummi. Long Charlie Wilson's son married a Lummi woman and brought her home to this village of Cape Mudge in the early days.

My wife Ida's family, the Dicks, used to go each summer to ṭaʔqa, now called Deepwater Bay, on the west side of Quadra Island. That was when her grandmother and grandfather were alive. It was real good fishing there.

Coming south from Deepwater Bay you pass through Seymour Na

rows and come into shore behind Yellow Island. That's where the old native village of qaẃicən was. But no people were there in my lifetime. There was fresh water there from a stream that lets out from Morte Lake above. It was a good fishing stream.

Near Maude Island there was a place where dangerous sea monsters were often sighted. Right in Seymour Narrows. We call that place ʔuʔstoy. One of these monsters always emerged around Maude Island. It must have been fifty feet across and always above its body, which looked like a great skate, there were little birds swirling round and round on the water. Everybody stayed away for fear of being dragged in and pulled under the water.

As a boy I fished up in Morte Lake. Old man Thulin, who was an early settler, had two donkey engines pulling logs down the west side of the river to the sea. Logging ruined that river for chums. Up in the lake Thulin had built a raft for fishing, and I caught sixty trout there in one hour. Ed Forrest, who lived at Quathiaski Cove, let out two hundred fathoms of line but never reached the bottom of Morte Lake.

Now I am going to tell you about one of the most important events to remember in the history of the We-Wai-Kai. It happened when we were staying in Gowlland Harbour on Quadra Island, before we moved to Campbell River and then to our present village at Cape Mudge. We called Gowlland Harbour and our location there ǧʷiǧʷakulis because of the whale we built there.[1] It is a good place, out of the southeast wind, open to the western sun. Passing canoes and ships on Discovery Passage couldn't see it because of headlands and islands.

Those old people built a whale and rigged it up with ropes so that it swam up and down in the water from our village in Gowlland Harbour the five hundred yards across to Stag Island. It was made from the skin of a blue whale supported by ribs of wood.

Four young chiefs got into that whale through the mouth, and they made it dive and surface again by rolling rocks from front to back and back again. The people who had the right to this would show it to the people at the potlatch. It looked like the whale's body was rising and sinking as it was pulled on the ropes four times across the water. We lost those four young men! They drowned in that whale on the third pass across the open water. Only halfway across the rope was cut. The whale sank with the weight of the rocks. It was sabotage! The rope was cut from the Stag Island side.[2]

It was in Gowlland Harbour that we had a big battle with the Haida. They came down this way, and our people were always watching out for them. We were warned that the Haida were coming. They used to

Plate 9
View of "Jumping-Down Place," a cliff Gowlland Harbour now occupied by Seascape Marine Chalets. Photo by Joy Inglis, 1984

watch on the cliffs up at Race Point for enemy canoes coming sout
through the narrows.

The battle took place on the cliffs we call həmx̌ʷəmax̌aʔas. Th
means jumping down. The Haida climbed up to the top of the blu
while our people hid back in the woods. Then we forced them to jum
down to their death. They were all killed. It was a big victory for th
people, and it has never been forgotten.[3] That cliff is on property wher
R. J. Walker used to live. He was the teacher from the Methodist Mi
sionary Society who came to Cape Mudge in 1893. There is a touris
resort on those cliffs today.

The Haida were the main threat to our people in the old times.
must have been a hundred years ago. Later, when we came to sett
Cape Mudge, we fortified the village, mostly against them. But gunboat
from Esquimalt fired on us here twice in the 1860's.[4] Cape Mudge wa
surrounded by a fence of logs laid horizontally with watch towers at th
four corners and holes in the log walls for firing guns. Quite a fe
Kwakiutl villages were like that in the early days. I think Tekya
Topaze Harbour was a fortified village.

When I was a boy, some of our people lived in and around Quathias
Cove. We call it gʷanusbaʔ. It means place on north side of point (fror

Figure 6
The Great Whale Ritual of the We-Wai-Kai people at Gowlland Harbour on Quadra Island. Illustration by Hilary Stewart, 1985

Cape Mudge). By the time I was born, the Pidcock brothers had sold their cannery there, but it was operated by others for a few years till it burned down in 1909. It was later rebuilt. When we were kids we used to walk the beach from Cape Mudge village to Quathiaski Cove over a trail at Whiskey Point to a little store that was built on the right hand side of the stream at the ferry landing. Before we learned English in school, we picked up quite a bit just listening to the people talking to each other in that store.

By early spring some of our people would be out at məx̌ənac (Mitlenatch Island), south of Quadra Island, gathering seagull eggs. I went there with my grandfather when I was just a little boy.

Half a mile outside the bell buoy south of Cape Mudge my grandfather was cod-fishing. In this place grandfather discovered a little man was hanging on his line. Just below the surface of the water the little man let go and slid off down the line to the bottom. There used to be a lot of bəgʷis. They live like us, only at the bottom of the sea. But they were small – maybe twenty inches long – and grandfather said that this little man had long hair and was hairy all over. It had two big front teeth. A lot of things were real then; we dance the bəgʷis these days with masks. Those bəgʷis must have moved off somewhere and are living now

re 7
ndfather catches a bəgʷis, Man-of-
ea. Illustration by Hilary Stewart,
5

in another part of the world.

Grandfather told me that his younger brother had part of the eye of
eagle rubbed on his own eyes when he was a baby. This gave him su
keen sight that when he looked into the water over the side of the can
he could see everything. Good for fishing! But grandfather said he s:
too much. He saw those kinds of beings that were under the surface
the water. By age fourteen he wouldn't go out of the house. He di
young.

The only way to reach Campbell River from our village was acr
Discovery Passage by boat, about a mile and three-quarters. I took
dugout canoe across when I was about ten years old. Every year a hu
headless monster used to jump out of the water just offshore fro
Campbell River below the big hill on Island Highway going south –
the direction of the forestry buildings. It was always in June on the
coming tide. It came every year through all the years I was growing
The last sighting was from Cape Mudge in 1957. All our people co
see it! It was the light golden colour of a sea lion. We called
wənd²isbalis, meaning sinking driftwood log, because that's what
looked like. It had no head or tail. It shot up out of the water and su
back in again. Some said it was a giant squid. It would have to be ov
grown all right for we could see it jumping all the way from Ca
Mudge! The last time I saw it, I was heading from Quathiaski Cove
Vancouver in my boat, and I passed by only five hundred yards away
was a monster four to five feet in diameter and forty feet long. It was
strong! It was leaping thirty feet into the air beginning in a northweste
direction and making a big circle about one-half mile round to where
started. Each jump was around one hundred feet from the last, anc
was moving fairly fast. No one sees it anymore. It must have mov
away some place. I think about that a lot because it must be living son
where in the seas. It must have moved off from here when the boat tr
fic got heavy.

On that Campbell River side of Discovery Passage there wasn't mu
of a white settlement when I was a boy. The Annex (hotel) was abc
where the Royal Bank is now. After that the Willows hotel was bu
There was a laundry run by Charley Thulin and a store where Lav
store was located, but it burned in 1917.

About that time there was prohibition, but traders and bootlegg
were selling liquor to our people in our villages on both sides of D
covery Passage. To get it under control, my father, Jim Smith, a
Francis Drake were made deputies. My father worked hard to keep
quor out of the villages. I never drank liquor when I was growing

even as a young man. I'll take a drink now with friends. That's about it. I have never been in a beer parlour.

In those early days there were whales of many kinds moving past our village in the passage between Cape Mudge and Campbell River, mostly blackfish but gray whales and humpies too. My own grandfather, Jim Naknakim, had this special understanding with whales. Once he was so sick he couldn't even walk any longer. As was the way with our people, he was put in a tent shelter by the shore. That was the way our people did it. It was healthy near the water, so you got better quicker. This was on the Campbell River spit, and my grandmother was with him, to help him. In the night there was a great splashing and whistling and blowing of whales, and about twenty of them came right in and ran up on the gravel shore.

Very early the next morning a young man appeared to my grandfather and asked, "Are you ready to go? There is a place for you with us." Grandfather was lying in bed very sick, but he wasn't old at that time, so he told the man that he was not ready to die yet, that he wanted to live. So the man said, "All right. Get yourself down to the water where you will find a spring salmon. Take it. Cut it into four slices, boil and eat it. You will be well."

Grandmother couldn't believe what was happening, but grandfather slid down to the water's edge on the beach pebbles, and there a salmon with no head (it had been bitten off by a whale for its own food) came swimming to the place where grandfather lay at the shore, the fins still moving. The whale was sharing its food with my grandfather. He ate the fish as the man had told him, and by the time he finished eating he was well again. So he knew that the man who had saved him had come from the whales. Those blackfish are human all right!

All Indians up and down the coast say that. If you talk to whales, they seem to understand. I have whistled to them and had them stand right up in the water. They rose three times straight up in answer to three whistles. Each time they answered me with a whistle. If you lie down in a boat they will come round whistling – calling – to you. In 1930 a man shot a blackfish. The others in the pod surrounded him in his boat. They lifted that boat up gently and placed it on the beach.

There was a really big storm here around 1917 – lightning, rain, thunder, wind. It went on and on for weeks. I remember coming down Seymour Narrows and watching the trees go up in flames with each lightning strike. A tree up above Cape Mudge village was struck. It sounded like an explosion. Rev. Rendle and his son Jack climbed up the hill behind the village with me to take a look at it. There was a hole four

Figure 8
The whales offer life with them to my
dying grandfather. Illustration by
Hilary Stewart, 1987

to five feet wide right through the tree, and its bark was torn off all the way round for seven feet. Whenever we heard these awful sounds of the storm, we always said kʷənkʷənxʷəlige, the Thunderbird![5]

This was the biggest and longest storm I remember. It happened like this: some Comox people were coming up this way, and just about the middle of Oyster Bay the wind got up. The trees were all moving and it started to thunder. From offshore in the canoes they could see the grasses near the beach being pushed apart and something huge moving there that had been disturbed. It was rising up and shaking the earth. Those people called it a snake, but it was much too big for that – it had a head as big as a horse and horns on it. It kept that storm going for almost a month. Those old people really saw those things. But nowadays they have gone off someplace else. Maybe they are in some other sea far away?

While we were in park in Honolulu, we saw these big birds coloured just like the hamatsa bird monsters we show in our dances. They were hopping from limb to limb, two feet together. Sometimes they swung their beaks back and forth. They sure looked like the big birds we show in our masks when the hamatsa dances. My wife Ida and I were laughing; we thought, "Hey, they must have moved over here to Hawaii!"

Grandfather told me about three men turned to stone. It was after the Flood. Three men were sitting there. I don't see them anymore, but they were there – big rocks – about one-quarter of a mile south of the Whisky Point reef on Quadra Island, facing south towards the village of Cape Mudge. I saw them myself when I was with grandfather. These men were sitting there and they must have said something bad to hełatusa, who came paddling down, fixing things as he came. His name means correct or right. He came to set the world right. He was like a god. So hełatusa said, "I'm going to turn you to rocks," and that's what happened. Those three rocks look like men. They were not far from a big rock shaped like a chesterfield that is still on the beach there today.

There are a lot of carvings on rocks on the beach in front of our Cape Mudge reserve, south of the lighthouse. Above the beach are sand cliffs, and on top is where Captain Vancouver met the Comox (1792). He visited ćakʷalotən, the village that used to be there. My daughter Audrey and son-in-law James Wilson were asked to meet "Captain Vancouver" out there in a ceremony they held in Centennial Year, 1967.

There must have been fifty rocks with carvings on them out on the beach below the old village.[6] Some people say petroglyphs were made by shamans. We called them pəx̌əla. Some of these shamans were here among our people, the Lekwiltok. We know who they were, but I won't

10
of the forty-four petroglyphs from
Cape Mudge foreshore (Site D1Sh-
his one, "Spirit Figure," is now
d by the ramp leading to the
Kiulth Museum. Photo by Erica
s, 1986

say their names. I don't want to talk about that! Well, you see, I do
really know about it because it was before my time.

When we were fishing up around Bella Bella and Bella Coola in t
1940's, we found out that people still believed in the power of shama
to kill whenever they want to. Maybe they still believe it! My own fatl
and mother believed in God, like I do. My mother used to say to m
about being harmed by witchcraft that if you don't believe it, nothi
will happen to you. "Put it out of your mind." She urged us to believe
the goodness of God. "That way you will always be among friend
They used to tell us, "If you think anyone is trying to get somethi
from you (to use in witchcraft), come straight to us and we will take ca
of it."

We respected those old people. They knew a lot. Ida and I reme
bered when we were around fourteen or fifteen years old, they wou
tell us "You better get up early! Never stay in bed! Fresh air is healt!
You will enjoy your life." We were told, "Get into the icy cold water.
have not done it, but I've seen it done myself. Old Siwis, he was Jo
Dick senior's father, when he was near one hundred years old, used
walk down to the beach here and dive in. My wife Ida used to like to
out in the canoe with him to fish. He was her uncle's father, and she
members that he was so old then that he couldn't pull on the oars I
just feathered them. His name Siwis means "noted man." He was rea
old when he went into that cold water.

4
Potlatch and Privilege

My earliest memory is of my father's great potlatch of 1911. My father, Billy Assu, worked for the money to give that potlatch for many years. He gave away goods and money to the value of more than ten thousand dollars. That was the biggest ever given here at Cape Mudge in those times. He became kʷikʷ, an eagle of the We-Wai-Kai, at that potlatch because he called in all fourteen tribes of the Kwagiulth.

His most important name was yax̌nəkʷaʔas (can give things away). It meant that people who want something come to him. This is a Village Island name given him by the people he was related to there. This name yax̌nəkʷaʔas came to me at a potlatch given to honour him two years after his death. Another name my father had was ozistalis. That name went to my brother Dan. He also held the name p̓aʔsəlał, meaning that he gives potlatches.

My father had many names. One of these, nəgedᶻi, meaning Big Mountain, was given to him by his father's brother, his Uncle Wamish, at a time when Wamish's oldest son had died. Wamish was a great chief of the Kwakwala-speaking people. His name meant "people going to dry fish on a beach by the river." It is a potlatch name meaning big provider.

At the time when my father gave this great potlatch of 1911, he already owned two very important ceremonies. The first of these is the Hamatsa Dance. It is shown in the early hours of the potlatch and is performed by the oldest son of the man giving the potlatch or by some other high-ranking relative.

The hamatsa is a man who has escaped from cannibal monsters and has returned home, but the cannibal spirit is on him and he is wild. He needs to be tamed. My father had the right to Hamatsa from his father-

in-law, Jim Naknakim, at the time he married my mother M
Naknakim. My mother's name was m̓axʷaʔuǧʷa. This means wealth. T
name Naknakim means (giving away) "from daylight to daylight."
grandfather Jim Naknakim's everyday name was ʔoyaca. It means gra
father, but it is used for men who are elders in the village.

The second important part of the potlatch that my father owned
ƛaʔsala. This can be spelled Klassila. He got that from the F
Ruperts. It was the original Klassila that first came down to the F
Ruperts from the Bella Bella people. The Chilkat blanket, headdre
and raven rattle that my father wore in the Klassila were never sold
taken away. The Klassila is the second part of the potlatch. I really like
Chiefs from all the tribes take part. They dance the Peace Dance w

Plate 11
Billy Assu and family inside his Big House at Cape Mudge, c. 1918. On the left are his sons Thomas and Frank. Billy Assu is in the centre, and his daughter Susan Quocksister is seated on his left, holding her son Herman. Standing behind her is daughter Lucy Chickite with her son Edward. Seated at the far right is Harry Assu. The photograph is from the Assu family collection (6775 CRMA). Courtesy of Bill and Brenda Assu.

ermine headdresses. Some are lured away outside the hall, and their λugʷe (treasure in the form of a privileged dance or supernatural being) comes back in their place. Only the Assu and Dick families at Cape Mudge had the right to the Klassila. The Dick family privilege probably came through marriage of my wife Ida's grandmother to bagʷani, a chief at Alert Bay.

I was only six years old when my father held his big potlatch, but I remember that nearly two thousand people were camped along the beach here at Cape Mudge. The people stayed for weeks. Many other smaller potlatches were given by others when everybody came here to my father's potlatch.

They dug a pit in the floor that was ten to twelve feet across. It was dug at night and hidden in the day. During the ceremonies one big sea monster we call sisiyuλ and six power boards came up from the pit.[1] The boards were made right here in the village by Johnny Klakwatsi of Salmon River. His name, Klakwatsi, means "big copper." He made most of the carvings at Cape Mudge in the early times, including my father's house posts and totem pole, and I used to watch him carving. Two pieces of two-by-twelve went across the pit to support the power boards as they unfolded and were pushed up from the pit by men hidden there. The pit was in front of where the drummers and singers sit at the back of the house, in front of the cloth screens. I wasn't frightened when I saw those huge beings appear. My uncle Mark had explained to me what was going to happen.

In 1913 Tom Wallace potlatched to all the Kwagiulth tribes. His son makmusa, Jim Wallace, was married to my father's sister Eliza. Tom Wallace was a big man at Cape Mudge then, and he was called on as "speaker" at the potlatches by our chiefs. Each village has a speaker for the chiefs. They do not need to be a high-ranking person, but Tom Wallace was a high-ranking man.

John Dick potlatched to all the tribes in 1913 too. He was my wife Ida's grandfather. Then, a year or two after that, Jim Naknakim potlatched to all the tribes. Jim Naknakim was my mother's father.

In my time, Wallace, Dick, Assu, and Naknakim were the ones to reach the position of Eagle because they went beyond calling the bands of the Lekwiltok tribe and called the people of all the tribes of the Kwagiulth. I hold the Eagle position from my father and in my own right.

I cannot say which of the leading men of the other bands of the Lekwiltok were Eagles. High-ranking men from these other bands usually came to Cape Mudge in winter to hold their potlatches, and some built

e 12
er board similar to those used
ng Billy Assu's potlatch of 1911.
one dates from the late nineteenth
ury and represents the supernatural
being Sisiutl. It is now in the
agiulth Museum at Cape Mudge.
o by Estelle Inman, 1986

Figure 9
John Dick, Sr., Memorial Pole at Cape Mudge. Drawn from early photographs by Hilary Stewart 1985

Plate 13 (opposite.)
Thunderbird crest on memorial to "Chief Cap. John Quak-sis-ta," head of the We-Wai-Kum tribe, who was buried at Campbell River in October 1902. (PN13413 RBCM)

houses here as well as in their own villages.

I remember four good-sized houses on the reserve at Campbell Rive. One belonged to George kʷaxsistala (Quocksister) who was the head man over there. Another belonged to Louie Gee. Johnny Galgome ha one. It was not a large house, but he gave a big potlatch. Quatell buil the last and biggest house. By the time the We-Wai-Kum moved the people down onto the spit at Campbell River, they weren't buildir many of the old-style houses any more. Quatell built his old-style hou for potlatching. Jim Smith, a We-Wai-Kum from Campbell River, bu: himself a house over here at Cape Mudge for potlatching.

At the Walitsum reserve at Salmon River Johnny Moon and his sc Moses were the leading men. Johnny Moon's name was maquilla. H died here at Cape Mudge in 1912 at a potlatch and is buried in o graveyard. Two years after the death of my mother in 1924, my fath married the widow of Johnny Moon. Her name kʷənxʷaʔugʷa mea: thunder. Charley Homiskinis and Chief Joe Roberts were high-rankir men at Salmon River. The late Georgie Dick's father, həmdᶻid, Kwaikah chief, was living up there when I was a boy. Joe Maundy, o of the Walitsum head men moved here to Cape Mudge and built a sm: modern house where Ruby Wilson's house now stands. Dave Moon, sc of Johnny Moon of Salmon River, married my cousin Daisy Naknaki and moved to Cape Mudge where his family still lives.

So far as my own family goes, we had lots of relatives in Cape Mud village because my grandmother on my father's side, ƛalapeniğa w one of four sisters. Her name meant to unfold valuables. Her sisters we Lottie Price, Norman Price's grandmother; Jimmy Hovell's moth Mary; and Nellie Cook's grandmother. The last was the only one move from our village. All these people were We-Wai-Kai. My fam has marriage connections with the people of Campbell River, Comc Salmon River, Alert Bay, Fort Rupert, and Village Island, and throu: these people our family connections spread even farther. Now we are lated to the Haida and Tsimshian in the north, the West Coast India on Vancouver Island, and the Salish to the east and south.

The important gifts at Lekwiltok potlatches were canoes. Everybo bought Hudson's Bay blankets, and these were used to buy canoes. T canoes were then given away to important people at our potlatch Blankets for exchange were bound ten to a roll with twine and heap up in a big pile for distribution.

My father gave away seventeen canoes at his potlatch in 1911. Sev of these were big: fifty-eight to sixty feet. The rest were around twen: six to thirty feet. Some big canoes were worth six hundred to seven hu

Plate 14
Part of the collection of Lekwiltok masks seized by the federal government in 1922. (6741 CRMA)

Plate 15
The Big Houses at Salmon River, c. 1910. Photograph by Edward Dosseter. (PN 2019 RBCM)

dred double-blankets, valued at about one dollar each. The cost depended mostly on the size of the canoe. Some canoes cost only two hundred blankets, with a downpayment of thirty-five.

People here used to buy into famous canoes even though they were no longer on the water and were even wrecked. Each canoe had a name and an owner, but people wanted to buy a share in those old canoes, and there was a lot of money invested in them. I remember that one was named máłap, which means white bottom. Another had a name meaning painted designs all over, but I can't remember the Kwakwala name for it.

Owning canoes that are gone is like owning big houses that are no longer standing. They are both valuable property. The ownership of my father's big traditional house and its carvings of crests passed on to me. I also own the sea-lion house named ƛixƛəx̌ilkʷ that once stood in Village Island. Jim Sewid gave me that house that belonged to his grandfather at my potlatch in 1979. Like some of the canoes at our potlatches, these big houses are not there any more, but their names, the posts, the right to their names, and everything else about them remains as a right of the family and will be passed down to my sons and grandsons. When you announce that at your potlatch it is like making a will!

When I was a boy, every high-ranking man here had a copper or had bought a share in a copper.[2] They probably came down the coast from the northern people. I know of a few coppers here that were obtained by marriage with the Alert Bay and Rivers Inlet people. In those early days white men in Victoria were making coppers with grooved sections and designs on them and selling them for one hundred and fifty dollars up along the coast.

At our early potlatches they tore Hudson's Bay blankets into strips, and these were thrown down from the rooftop for a scramble. Our women sewed the strips together on the sewing machine and then wore the blankets made from them. The scramble was lots of fun, and the blankets made of strips given at the potlatch were worth more than ordinary blankets.

At my father's potlatch nułəmała was danced. A mask is worn and there is a lot of clowning. My uncle Jack Naknakim could perform that. He kept order for the Hamatsa with a big club with a spiked round end. Only the Naknakim and the Long Charlie (Wilson) family had the rights to used that kind of club. Then in the following days during Klassila father danced the Peace Dance, and all the family took part in dancing all the masks to show the people. The potlatch was held for many days in a row back then, at least for four days. Now it is all held in one afternoon and evening.

I remember a big carved wood frog displayed at my father's potlatch that I really liked as a little boy. The fun of seeing this frog is my first memory in life. Our name for frog is waʔqes. I think that that frog may have sat up in a cradle where you would not expect to see it. When the tuʔxʷid danced, bending her knees down low to the fast beating of the boards, the frog would sit up in the cradle and whistle without her ever touching it. We called the tuʔxʷid lady dancer. She is a mysterious person wearing hemlock branches who has gone around the world to find a treasure of magic powers. She claims to be pregnant. The old people tease her to prove it and finally she produces some marvellous trick, like

Plate 16
Whistling Frog carved in wood. It is painted and has glass marble eyes. Used in the potlatch of Billy Assu in 1911, it was among the items seized in 1922. It was sold by the government to collector George G. Heye and is now in the Museum of the American Indian. (11/5185)

that frog that whistled up out of a baby cradle. It is likely that Jimmy Wallace's wife would have been father's tuʔxʷid dancer. She was my father's oldest sister, a woman of high rank, with the right to perform it.

Later in life I saw a frog like the one I remember pulled across the big house floor by the tuʔxʷid dancer at a potlatch at Fort Rupert. So now I am not sure which was the way it was shown here by my father.

That big frog was bought by a collector from the stuff that was being taken away from our people so they couldn't potlatch. We want those things given back. My nephew Bill Assu and Bob Joseph and others for the two museums at Alert Bay and here went down to New York to talk to those people, but nothing has come out of it. Earlier on we asked them to photograph my father's frog carving and send that to us. At first

Plate 17
Thirty-five-foot high "fish trap" platform built for Wallace's potlatch in 1913 is seen at the centre of this photograph. The first modern house at Cape Mudge, built in 1894, can be seen through the supports of the platform. Harry Assu was born there in 1905. Photo by Trio Crocker (11708 RBCM)

*Figure 10.
Dan Assu Memorial Pole carved by
Jimmy King. Erected at Cape Mudge in
1955. Drawing by Hilary Stewart,
1985*

they said they didn't know anything about it and couldn't find it, but after a few months they sent us the picture for this book.

In 1917, when father put up a potlatch for the four bands of the Lekwiltok tribe – Salmon River, Campbell River, Phillips Arm, and Cape
Mudge – he made every one of us sons and daughters dance: three sons
and two daughters. That's the first time my sisters Lucy and Susan were
called to dance with us boys. We wore button blankets, aprons, headdresses with eagle down, and we formed a line to dance the Peace
Dance.

The potlatch I really remember best is the one given when I was
twelve years old by my grandfather, Jim Naknakim. Before the potlatch
they dug a hole twenty feet in diameter in the big house floor where his
son, my uncle Jack, went down and was hidden. He was hamatsa. When
he came out at the potlatch, he was wild. I knew that pit well. When
they were digging it, a fellow from Fort Rupert who was helping out
grabbed me, and just for fun he tumbled me down into it. When the
men finished digging out the hole they put in two-by-fours all along
vertical, to keep the earth from caving in on Jack's body. They must
have buried a rope too because this guy was holding the rope that
dragged my uncle Jack up out of the pit.

Tom Wallace, the high-ranking man who gave his potlatch to all the
tribes in 1913, had a big totem pole standing in front of his house.[3] His
potlatch name was ṗadᶻiyus, meaning "spring melt" or "high river." He
had a platform thirty-five feet high built outside the front of his big
house for his biggest potlatch. You reached it with a ladder. I saw his
youngest son, Jack Wallace, dance Hamatsa on that platform. It was the
only time I saw a body carved out of wood used in the cannibal
ceremony here. The platform he danced on would be around three feet
wide by seven feet long – like a table. The ladder and platform were
made right in the village, built to look like part of the fish trap then in
use on the Little Bear River near Rock Bay in Johnstone Strait. The ladder on the real trap stretched from shore out to a platform where men
stood to look down into the trap to see if the salmon were in. The platform stood for a long time out in the village street, long after Tom Wallace's house burned down. Some old people have said that the platform
in the street was used for making speeches. Some said it was used for
calling out names of those getting blankets at potlatch.

Mungo Martin of Fort Rupert spent months here at Cape Mudge carving the masks to be used in my father's potlatch of 1911. He worked in a
shed that was set up beside my grandfather's big house, which was still
standing then. My father got the rights from the Fort Ruperts to many of

the dances he showed at his big potlatch. So many masks were shown that they stretched right around the whole big house. Our family got together with the Fort Ruperts when my father and George Hunt wanted to marry their son and daughter. The eldest son in our family was Dan, and he was married to George Hunt's daughter Grace. Dan was fourteen years old. Grace, Tommy, and Agnes Hunt were all children of George Hunt and his wife Abayah. When George died, Abayah was married to Mungo Martin. Dan and Grace didn't have to live together. They understood that. This kind of marriage we called xʷisa. It is a way to bring families together and exchange wealth and rights. It was through marriage that people got the rights to masks and songs and dances in those early days. It was by making good marriages that these things got spread out through the tribes. That's how it worked. People who were high married into a high family.

We were four brothers: Dan, myself, Frank, and Thomas. My father looked into who we should marry to give us the best chance. Daughters, too. My sisters Lucy and Susan were married into high families. My sister Lucy, the eldest, was married to Johnny Chickite of Cape Mudge. My sister Susan was married to Johnny Quocksister of the We-Wai-Kum of Campbell River.

When my father first went up to Fort Rupert, he gave a potlatch there. In a couple of months all the Fort Ruperts came down, and there was a potlatch here when they brought down their masks to show the old people how to dance them. My father told me: "When you grow up you are going to do the same thing arranging for the marriages for your children." But when the potlatch dropped here, things changed.

My father had a local We-Wai-Kai song-maker named Long Charley (Wilson) compose and teach the songs for him. My own father was a very good singer. He sings some of his songs on a record by Ida Halpern. She came up and stayed here in my house for the opening of the Kwagiulth Museum in 1979 and brought me the record.[4]

My marriage to Ida Dick (1907–1983) was arranged when we were children. Ida was the only daughter of Major Dick. Her father died when she was four. He was the son of John Dick senior, who was a head man of that family. Ida's mother, Mary Dick, died when Ida was seven. She was raised by her grandmother, Mary Anne Smith of the We-Wai-Kum band of Campbell River, and her father's sister, Lizzie Dick of Cape Mudge. (Lizzie Dick later married Charley Peters of Salmon River.) When I was around twelve years old, my mother told me that I would be marrying Ida when I was old enough. Ida was told too. We just took it for granted. We were good friends, living just a few houses away from each other. We were both from high-ranking families, and it just seemed to be the right thing for us to do. When it came time for the marriage of my own sons and daughters, the arrangements were made in the Christian church in the way it was for those times.

I went up to Alert Bay for a potlatch in 1978 when Jimmy Sewid's daughter Daisy and her husband Lorne Smith, who had been married for a long time, were married again in the Indian way. Jim Sewid announced for me that all the people were invited to my potlatch the next year to celebrate the raising of a memorial pole to my father inside the Kwagiulth Museum at Cape Mudge. When you raise a pole, you have to potlatch. The pole in the museum is my father's original pole that used to stand in front of his big house in Cape Mudge, but now it is carved

Plate 18
Ida Assu (1907–1983), wife of Harry Assu. Ida was the daughter of Major Dick. Her marriage to Harry was arranged when they were children.

again. He told me after the old pole went to Johnny Quocksister's father in a marriage arranged for my sister Susan that if a pole was ever put up again it should be that one. My sons and I asked Sam Henderson of Campbell River and his sons to carve the pole, and it was put up inside the museum.

At the potlatch at Alert Bay when my potlatch was announced. Tommy Hunt from Fort Rupert was sitting beside me and he said to me, "You're going to potlatch? Klassila, because you have that!"

I said, "That's what I'm going to use: Klassila, and Hamatsa, because we have both."

Hunt said, "I'll dance that." He and his brother William Hunt danced Klassila here at my potlatch. I gave away goods and money, and in all this potlatch cost me around fifteen thousand dollars.

My son-in-law James Wilson potlatched that night, too. He is originally from Kingcome Inlet but is a member of the Cape Mudge Band. My daughter Audrey, his wife, danced Kingcome style with paper money sewed on her cedar-bark headdress and paper money pinned all down her blanket.

The old people who gave the big potlatches in Cape Mudge that I remember worked all year round, summer and winter, to make money to potlatch. My father was fishing for the company in Quathiaski Cove in the spring and summer, and in the fall he went to a place east of Frederick Arm on the Mainland where he stayed all winter logging. He did that for five years to help make money for his biggest potlatch. But he was working toward that potlatch for eight to ten years.

Our family went with him to the logging claim to help, and his brother Mark worked with him in the hardest work. Tom Price and Jim Hovell of Cape Mudge had claims there too. They all sold the logs to Fred Bukar, who had a camp near Yaculta Rapids. Men were working in this way in those days to make enough money to call the fourteen tribes to a potlatch and raise their family up high.

There's a big mountain up there next to Frederick Arm that we call potlamin (Mt. Estero). While we were up there logging, we would see this single bird every morning – sitting out on a point of land along the beach only three to four hundred feet from us. It was a qulus. It was covered with white downy feathers. It was snow white. And it was bigger than an eagle and had a nice long yellow beak, maybe seven inches long. Every morning this qulus took off and flew up into the high mountains, making a rumbling noise like thunder that made my hair stand on end! I saw it over and over. We don't see them any more. They must have gone away someplace else. It was a qulus all right. I saw it over and over again.

The people of old, before my father's time, only worked hard in the summer, and that's when they made enough goods to last for the year. And whoever was going to give the potlatch in the winter... that was where they were going! That is our time to get together to show all our dances.

In those days that's the way they were looking forward to passing the winter time. That's the way I look at it. Today, our people especially, what are they doing in winter time? Just sitting there looking at T.V. Nothing! That T.V. can make a lazy people of you!

The people of Cape Mudge at one time all lived in the old style houses of beams, with cedar board roof and sides. They were, on average, forty

Plate 19
Six village boys sitting in feast dishes, c. 1919. From left to right they are Johnny Wilson, Ernest Price, Herman Quocksister (nephew of Chief Harry Assu), Bill Roberts, Norman Price, and Johnny Wilson's younger brother. May Henderson Collection (1038 CRMA)

by sixty feet. There were about ten of them stretching along the seafront at Cape Mudge.

Each big house belonged to a different chief, and all his family and relatives lived together. My grandfather, Charley Assu, owned a big house. His name kəmqoḷas means coming together (for the potlatch). I don't remember his wife, my grandmother. She died when I was four years old.

My father had already built himself a modern home at Cape Mudge long before he put up his big house in 1910 for his big potlatch. When my father's house went up, my grandfather's old house was pulled down. It wasn't big enough to hold the fourteen tribes at a potlatch.

By the time I can remember the village, around seventy-five years ago,

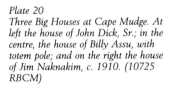

Plate 20
Three Big Houses at Cape Mudge. At left the house of John Dick, Sr.; in the centre, the house of Billy Assu, with totem pole; and on the right the house of Jim Naknakim, c. 1910. (10725 RBCM)

most families had a little house on the waterfront out in front of their big house. They are shown on a map in the Kwagiulth Museum made by Charley Peters, who was Walitsum from Salmon River. He married Lizzie Dick of Cape Mudge and moved to Cape Mudge. That old beach front shown on his map seems to have been washed away by tides and winter storms.

At the top of the map you can see the place where the women used to wash their clothes in a stream that came down there from the hillside behind the church. When they put a new pump house for the village in at that place last year, the workmen digging the trenches for the pipes found human bones. Indian people have been living on the site of our village for thousands of years.[5]

An important man named peʔdᶻədᶻiyem (Fitzgerald) lived in the house of Long Charley Wilson. In 1907, he called all those living on the Campbell River, We-Wai-Kum and Kwaikah, and let them know that they could remain there so long as we were not using it, but they should leave our buildings over there alone. I was only a small boy at that time.

I was born in 1905 in the first modern house at Cape Mudge, built by my father in 1894. It was his idea to acquire the new style of house. He always wanted to improve, to go ahead, to modernize. My father and the men in the village had put up this kind of house when they built a house with milled lumber for Mr. Walker, the missionary teacher, and his family for their arrival in 1893. So when my father decided to build the new style house for his family in 1894, everybody pitched in to help him. The house was built at the north end of the village.

The modern home my father built is shown on the left-hand side of the map, well back from the beach and in a line with other houses that were built later when the village modernized. It was a good-sized house with four bedrooms, living-room, and kitchen. Seventeen years later, when my father decided that he would put up one of the big traditional houses for his potlatch, there was no objection from our ministers. They came to watch our potlatches and enjoyed them.

Each family called the people to potlatch in their own house. There was no separate "potlatch house" in the village. Now, quite a few villages have one big house for potlatching, and we are planning to build one here at Cape Mudge. Modern houses are too small to hold the number of people who come to a potlatch.

In the old family houses at Cape Mudge the floor was dug down about three feet deep inside to keep out the draughts. The earth in the floors was mixed with clay from our hillside to keep down dust. A four-foot-high bench for sitting and sleeping ran around the sides and across the end farthest away from the door. The doors were placed in the end of the house looking over the sea. There was one big smoke hole in the roof.

People could sit and sleep on the wide benches. But there were rooms built into the four corners of the house too. I remember it so well. All the masks and things were stored there, and my brothers and I used to sneak in and put on the masks and regalia when we were really just kids. Once we got into the stuff and went running outside to our friends to show off. Those things were never to be worn except by the people who had the rights to them, and only at potlatches. My father came down hard on us that time. It makes me laugh to think of it now, but back then... oh, how we got spanked!

Our big houses didn't have paintings on the front face so far as I know, although there were painted house fronts in the village of Salmon River. There were carved house posts holding up the beams of the houses at Cape Mudge. Those from my father's big house built in 1910 are in the museum in Ottawa. They stood twenty feet high. Two figures were carved on each post. hux̌ʷhuqʷ, a bird that is part of the Hamatsa Dance, was on top, and beaver below. A crossbeam of the house holding up the roof crossed between those posts. Most of the logs for the beams and posts came from Phillips Arm on the Mainland where my father had been logging timber and had brought out the best. Oh it was beautiful big cedar! The posts holding up the roof at the back of the house were carved and painted, but other posts and beams were just polished off. The front of the building was milled lumber from a sawmill in Quathiaski Cove. We called the big planks split for the roof "shakes." The logs had been floated into the village, cut with a saw to eight-foot lengths, and split with yew-wood wedges to two-inch thickness. My father figured it took over a thousand of these sheets to cover the framework. They went for one dollar a shake in those days; so my father lost a lot when he pulled down that big house. That house and all the rights to crests connected with it have come down to me by hereditary right.

My father's totem pole stood out in front of his big house. The whale is a crest that came in from the Naknakim side of my family when my father married my mother. The eagle at the top indicates my father's position as an eagle of the We-Wai-Kai. The pole is the one returned to the Kwagiulth Museum from the Calgary Zoo after seventy years, and it is in storage there for the time being.

In John Dick's big house there were three big welcome figures, two near the entrance and one in the middle at the back. They belonged to his son Major Dick, who was my wife Ida's father. The carved posts welcome the people to the potlatch. When Major Dick died in 1913, John Dick was still alive, and one year later he potlatched in his son's memory and gave away a thousand blankets. This was shown on the copper above the head of one of the carved men on these posts. They were later put out on the beach near where the old gravehouses used to be. One figure has a copper on his chest, showing that the chief had a copper; one holds his stomach, and that means he gave feasts; and one figure is calling. It shows he called the people to a potlatch.[6] The museum at Campbell River took them over to preserve them and one fell apart, but the two that were still all right were given back to the Kwagiulth Museum at Cape Mudge when it opened in 1979.

Today at Cape Mudge, there are five totem poles, five welcome fig-

Plate 21
James Hovell and the Rev. G. Knox stand beside three Potlatch Welcoming Figures belonging to Major Dick, son of John Dick, Sr., c. 1930. "Copper"-shaped boards placed sideways on the posts announce the number of blankets given away by the host. Des Maris Collection (8710 CRMA)

ures, a painting on the community hall, and the potlatch regalia in the Kwagiulth Museum that was taken away from our people in 1922 and was only returned to us in 1979 after years of struggle to get back what is ours.

In those early days, my father was chief of the village of Cape Mudge. The government expected one man to speak for his people in each village, and he was held responsible for the actions of all the people.

George Pidcock was magistrate in Courtenay in the 1930's, and once when I was going down there, my father asked me find out how old he had been at the time he became chief of Cape Mudge Village. George Pidcock was the son of Reg Pidcock (died 1902), who used to be Indian agent at Quathiaski Cove and a great friend of my father. They had helped each other all they could in every way. Magistrate Pidcock told me, "Your father was the youngest chief on this coast ever to be elected to that position. I remember that he was twenty-four years old at the time because we are the same age, and I was twenty-four at the time he was elected."

It was our custom that the heads of each big family that we call ṅaṁima worked for their own. There were five or six of these families at Cape Mudge. My father was high in the ṅaṁima called giẍʷsəm, which means chiefs. Each head of the family worked hard to raise up his family in the potlatch and do whatever he could for the people of the village. It was good. It worked for everybody.

But times around here were rapidly changing. My father was the chief for Cape Mudge, and he felt that there were new opportunities for his people. The big chance came in 1919 when our people formed a company to log timber on our reserve at Drew Harbour. The band made twenty-three thousand dollars. I was a whistle-punk, making nine dollars a day. That was a big wage in those days when white men were getting around three dollars a day in the logging camps. We shared all the money we made, so that's when we got modern homes in the village of Cape Mudge.

The big potlatches at Cape Mudge were dropped, but of course families were potlatching in their own homes. For all the time my father represented our village, the pressure was put on chiefs by the government and the church at Alert Bay to abolish the potlatch or go to jail. Alert Bay was the centre for that.

My father called all the people together and told them, "We have made good money so we can modernize the village. We are going to do it now. There will be modern homes for each family, an electric power plant and waterworks." At this important meeting, the old men who had tried to stop changing with the times spoke up and said, "We are with you. We know it is better to change." Some people who remember how fast the white people seemed to be moving in on us at the time say, "If you can't beat them, join them!"

My father told the people, "We are going to tear down the big houses and build modern homes." He told them that the times were changing and that this was the opportunity to change with them. People wanted it because they were anxious to get going on the new plan for the village.

In mid-April of 1920 they brought the two donkey engines around from our Drew Harbour operation and started in to level the land beginning at both ends of the village. Three big houses in good condition were standing then – Dick, Assu, and Naknakim. A few others were in poor repair. All these old-style houses were knocked down, and the boards were cleaned up on the beach by burning.

Four big government shovels were brought in to level the ground where the dug-out floors inside the big houses had been. The area levelled off is the open area in the village from the bus shelter to the swimming pool. The big houses had extended even farther back from the sea than this grassy strip. They covered the road that is closest to the water and were partly under the homes that stretch in a long row facing Discovery Passage.

We figured we had done the right thing. As it turned out, we did do the best thing! We have a modern village that has been said to be the finest native village in British Columbia by people who know. And we are building up our traditions and holding the big potlatches again. So it has been good in both ways: modern and traditional. People from the other Indian villages who come here to visit or for the potlatch have told me, "You are way ahead." Well, that didn't just happen you know! We worked hard for that!

In some native villages up and down the B.C. coast the leaders are only now trying to get good housing for their people and modern servicing. They were slower to modernize. They speak well of Cape Mudge village when they come here to our potlatches.

It wasn't easy for my father to lead his people into a new way of life. He was so young when he was chosen to represent his people, and for a long time a few of the old guys worked against the new ways and opposed him. But the most important people supported my father, and, finally, when a real chance came to take advantage of the changing times, people were all for it.

5
My Life in the Fishing Business

The seiner on the old Canadian five-dollar bill was my boat at the time the photograph for the engraving was taken in 1958. We were in Johnstone Strait at the time. Ripple Point can be seen on the right, and Knox Bay Point is shown on the left. I had been running her for eighteen years at the time. I owned the *BCP 45*, having bought her from B.C. Packers in 1941. I don't really know why my boat was chosen, but when I asked the president of the company that question later, he said, "You fished for the company for a long time and were a good fisherman for the company in all those years." At that time I was the oldest skipper in the fleet. I worked for B.C. Packers for forty-nine years. Well, that's a lot of fish brought in for the company all right. I was never low boat, always better than average catch each year. My son Mel skippered the *BCP 45* for me, and I ran the *W9* for the company. I sold *BCP 45* back to the company in 1959 and bought the *W8* from them.

Plate 22
The old Canadian five-dollar bill with an illustration of the seiner once owned by Harry Assu, BCP 45, *on the back. In the background is the* Bruce Luck, *which was owned by Steve and Don Assu.*

There were two Assu boats on the five-dollar bill. In the background of the engraving of my boat on the bill, you can see the *Bruce Luck*. My sons Steve and Don owned the *Bruce Luck*. Don skippered her, and Steve ran another boat for the company.

It has been really nice having my old boat on the five-dollar bill. Once when Ida and I were flying to Hawaii for a holiday, the pilot came back to speak to us. We had holidayed often in Hawaii, but this was the first time the pilot had talked with us. Maybe it was because there were so many of our family at the airport to see us off. He wanted to know who we were. He asked me what I did for a living, and I told him I was a fisherman. Ida said, "Show him your boat," so I pulled out a Canadian five-dollar bill. He returned to his cabin and announced to the passengers that we were on our fiftieth wedding anniversary and that my fishing boat could be seen on the five-dollar bills in their pockets. The stewardesses were soon changing American money and larger Canadian bills into fives, and I was kept busy all the way to Hawaii signing them for the passengers. I signed one hundred and forty-five bills! We all had a lot of fun.

Recently a CBC camera crew came up to photograph me on the *BCP 45* in the same waters near Kanish Bay where the original picture was taken nearly thirty years ago. It was shown later on television, and it looked pretty good on the screen though the boat has become run-down over the years. It used to be a table-seiner, but now it is fitted with a drum. *BCP 45* is still in these waters. It has changed hands over the years. Allen Chickite bought her in 1983 from the company. He took her down for a boat parade at the opening of EXPO '86 in Vancouver. About seven seiners from Cape Mudge went down to join in the opening.

My very first boat was a dug-out canoe made of cedar. My father bought it for me from Oscar Lewis's father, who steamed and bent it in the old steaming shed in our village. There were a lot of canoes at Cape Mudge then, drawn up along the shore near the houses. Different styles of cedar canoes were the only boats our people used. I remember four sixty-foot-long canoes drawn up at the north end of our village when I was a boy.

I caught a lot of fish from that little twelve-foot canoe fitted with oars. I'd take my canoe out in the morning and fish in the pass for salmon with just a hand-line and bring in a twelve- to fifteen-pound salmon. Then out in the evening again, and come in with maybe twenty fish. There were so many fish in Discovery Passage then you could walk on them! I got paid fifty cents cash for each spring salmon at the cannery at

Quathiaski Cove.

When we were young and the water was filled with salmon, we used to get them with our hands right out of the gravel on the beach in front of our village. My brother Frank and I caught coho that were chasing the herring up the beach. The beach would be covered with "snake herring," we called them, that got buried four or five inches deep in the gravel by the surf. The salmon swarmed in after them, and we clubbed them. One afternoon we got thirty-five at low-slack tide. Every year in August we got coho that way. They were pretty well full-size by then. The scow from the cannery called in at the village, and we got fifteen cents each for coho.

Our people had always hand-lined from canoes, and we took fish in traps in the mouth of the rivers. So far as I know, it was only after non-Indians came that we fitted our canoes with oars and sail.

We got paid for our fish around here for the first time when Pidcock brothers opened their cannery in Quathiaski Cove in 1904. We continued to troll by canoe for the company right up to the time that W. E. Anderson took over as manager in 1912. After that we began to drag-seine, setting a net off the beach. We did that here in front of our village, in the mouth of the Campbell River on the spit, and at the mouth of the Nimpkish River. The Nimpkish band owned that northern area but allowed others to use it. I worked with Dan Cranmer on the drag-seine up there. It was heavy work. Boy there was a lot of fish! We took sockeye that way from around June first to mid-July.

My father bought the first gas boat here at Cape Mudge in 1912. Within two or three years everybody here at Cape Mudge had been able to buy a gas boat with money we were paid for our fish. They could see the advantage of this type of boat. My father always urged saving and planning for our people. He told us boys to be looking ahead two or three years to what boat would give us the best return and to save our money to get it. That way our people grew up in this fishing business and always kept ahead and are successful in it.

When the first cannery men came to this coast, they put up the canneries at places where our people were living – at the best salmon rivers – and we knew how to take the fish in our own waters. The cannery managers needed the Indian men to bring in the fish and women to work in the canneries. It was good. We were working together, co-operating. Later when other people got into the fishing business, we had to fight for our place in it.[1] We have to fight for our place in it even today! Of course, we were working in other kinds of industry that were coming in. Pidcock brothers owned a logging company in Gowlland

Harbour and Sam Lewis, Soloman, and Jack Naknakim from Cape Mudge worked there. There were other lines of work. Furs brought in money: weasel, mink, coon, and bear. Around 1914 I did quite a bit of otter-hunting for skins up at Otter Cove south of Chatham Point. In the 1920's there was a bounty on cougars. Jack Naknakim and Francis Drake were cougar hunters.

When I was around seventeen years old, my father helped my brother Dan and me to get hold of an old gill-netter. We rebuilt it – cabin, deck, engine, everything. We ran it for about three years, and everybody in the village could use it if they needed it. They didn't have to ask. That's the way it used to be back then – really nice, just like one family. If you stepped outside your house to chop wood, four or five guys would come along with saws to help you. There is hardly any of that left in the village today. When my family got the very first telephone in the village, we left the door of the house open so that everybody could come in and use it.

There were still many of our traditions left in my boyhood. It must have been around 1914 when we were coming back from gill-netting around Steveston and I was on my father's boat. It was fall, and about thirty of our boats were pinned down in Baker Passage in a big storm. The wind and waves prevented us from putting out to cross the Strait of Georgia to our village at Cape Mudge. We anchored there two or three days waiting for the wind to die down. Finally, the men said, "Now we are going to start the wind we need to take us home." They rolled logs down the beach to the shore and made a raft. They set a fire burning on the raft and shoved it out into the Strait. That calmed the wind that was against us, and we made it home to Cape Mudge.

In the old cannery days the fish were everywhere in great numbers. Not like it is today. All those little mainland creeks and rivers had their runs. In Topaze Harbour the dog salmon ran up the river just north of our old village of Tekya, and coho ran in the river just south of the village. Coho went into Loughborough Inlet in August, and sockeye came into the inlet at Heydon Bay near the reserve at Homayno. I'd be about seventeen years old that time I went into Loughborough Inlet with my skipper McPherson and got permission from Loughborough Bill, who owned those waters, to fish in there. We made one set and brought in five thousand fish. A big logging camp ruined the fishing at Loughborough after that. Stocks are only now building up again.

My father was recruiter for native workers at the cannery at Quathiaski Cove. He called Indian people around Ladysmith and arranged for them to stay on our reserve south of the village. Even after the cannery burned down, they came each summer from Ladysmith and while the men fished, the women spun wool and knitted Cowichan sweaters. They were still coming every year in the 1960's. Most of the native men and women working for the cannery were from Cape Mudge, but some at Comox with relatives in our village came up to work with us, and a few were from Campbell River and Salmon River. A recruiter was paid so much for each worker signed on by him, and my father was held responsible for the workers in Quathiaski Cove cannery. He represented their rights in any dispute.

Aluminum tokens were given to us as payment for our fish at the cannery, and during the canning season they could only be cashed at the company store. Our people didn't like that, and so my father put a stop to it. The metal coins were taken off in the 1920's, and after that when our catch was brought in, the amount of fish was recorded in the "fish book." We were paid off in cash at the end of the season. That money was real money and could be spent anywhere, but my father urged people to save, not spend.

In those days quite a few loggers and fishermen blew everything they had at the end of the season. There was a lot of that. We had a joke about "going in the hole." You know, "Quathiaski Cove" is a Comox word meaning a bay with an island in the mouth, but to us it sounds like

Figure 11
The large chamber-pot-shaped rock at Whiskey Point, Quadra Island, located by Gerrie Dinsley and Pauline Dowler, volunteers at the Kwagiulth Museum, Cape Mudge, on information from Harry Assu, in 1988. Sketch by Hilary Stewart, 1989

a word in Kwakwala that means "piss-pot." There really is a big roc
bowl in the Cove just off Whiskey Point. Well anyway, when Sandy Bill
was fishing up at Rivers Inlet and his wife Mary was working in the car
nery at Quathiaski Cove, and any one asked Sandy how Mary was h
would always say: "Oh, she's in the hole at Quathiaski Cove!"

On the tenth of August 1921, my father called a meeting of ou
people with the cannery manager on the wharf at Quathiaski Cove. W
had no quarrel with management; we wanted a federal governmen
regulation changed so that native men could be seine-boat skippers. U
to then only white men and Japanese men could be seine-boat skipper
Yet Indians were top fishermen, and the company was in favour c
giving us this right. They did not want to stand in our way. W. E. Ander
son, part-owner and manager, was a close friend of my father and one c
the finest men I ever knew. Bill Nye, the foreman, was married to my fa
ther's sister Pauline. It was like a family.

Allan W. McNeill, M.P. for Comox-Alberni, was at that meeting o
the wharf, and he offered to take our grievance to Ottawa. Word cam
back that Indians could skipper seine boats. My father was a good seine
boat skipper, sure was! That first year he took the seine boat into Log
gers Bay, two miles north of Deepwater Bay in Discovery Passage. That
a big deep pool where migrating salmon move slowly in and out agair
He had the deepest net and my skipper, a Scotsman named McPherson
was sure he was going to snag it. Well, he never did. He pulled in ove
four hundred thousand salmon in one season – June to Septembe
Nearly half a million fish! There sure were lots of fish back then, and m
father knew where the fish were going to hit.

The company had around five seine boats at the time, and my fathe
arranged that where the skipper was not Indian, two native men woul
be taken on in every crew of six. That was when I was first taken on a
crew on a seine boat along with Harry Moon, the son of the rankin
chief at Salmon River. We all got along fine. McPherson was our skippe
They were all fine men. They used to laugh and call us "sunburne
Scotsmen"! It always makes me laugh to think about it.

Every boat had a Chinese cook, and on our boat we had a man name
Ying, who had cooked in the Hotel Vancouver. We didn't have hir
long, you bet! When W. E. Anderson learned about it, Ying was take
off our boat to cook for the Anderson family.

As well as Chinese who were cooks on the boats, there was a cre
that came up from Vancouver every summer to work the cannery. The
gutted and cut the fish into slices that fit the tins. Some of these men cu
tins from metal sheets three feet by two feet. Then they soldered then

Later machines replaced the slicer and automatically made the cans. The machine that replaced hand-slicing was called the Iron Chink. There was a bunk house at Quathiaski Cove near the cannery that they stayed in, and we called it "Chinee House." In the evening we'd see them there playing cards and passing the pipe.

The Japanese who had been mainly building boats and fishing on the Fraser River from their village in Steveston began settling in large numbers in places further north along the coast and on the west coast of Vancouver Island. Before the 1920's men of the Japanese families around here worked in the lumber camps at Duncan Bay and Loughborough Inlet. Starting around 1916, fishermen from Steveston began coming up here in spring for the cod-fishing. It must have been around 1918 or 1919 that I began to notice the very large number of their boats cod-fishing. I counted thirty-nine of their boats in Quathiaski Cove on one day.

Almost all the boats used by the cannery at Quathiaski Cove were Japanese owned, built, and run. In 1922 when they brought in the regulation permitting our people to skipper seine boats and crew on boats skippered by others, some regulations were applied to Japanese boats. That was when the company began chartering Japanese seine boats. The skipper stayed on, but it allowed the company to hire other people on the seine boats for crew. In the case of skippers for herring seining, a Japanese could only skipper if he was a veteran, and half the crew had to be Indian or no licence would be issued. The company chartered the gill-netters and cod-boats of the Japanese with no restriction on captain or crew.

I worked with the Japanese once when I was twenty-one years old, in 1926. I signed on in Nanaimo to go herring seining for the saltery on Gabriola Island. They dry-salted the fish and shipped it to Japan. They had another big operation on Saltspring Island and another on Blind Channel near Phillips Arm. I worked for the Matsuyama Company on a fifty-five-foot seiner. We used to sing together as we brailed in the fish: "Yu-Mara-Yu, Yu-Nara-Yu." It was really nice. Had a real tune and beat to it! I asked them why they did that, and they told me it makes the work go better. They were good to work with. Everybody working together. A hard-working people all right! Work is nothing to them.

After crewing with McPherson as my skipper for a few years, I went on my Uncle Jimmy Hovell's boat for a season. It was *Annandale*, the first boat he ever skippered. The very first seiner I ever skippered was *Quathiaski 8*. The boat belonged to the company operation at Quathiaski Cove. I was around twenty-nine years old at the time.

I've owned quite a few boats over my lifetime as a fisherman. I owned a gill-netter named *Gildees*. That's our name for a long beach in Johnstone Strait. The *Gildees* was built right here in Cape Mudge Village by John Dick. It was a standard size: about thirty-two feet long. After that I had a gill-netter, *Jean A.*, named for my daughter, wife of Tom Roberts, chief councillor of the Campbell River band. I built the frame of the *Jean A.*, and Robert Clifton planked her. Then in 1941 I bought the *BCP 45*. That's the one on the five-dollar bill.

During the depression years of the 1930's, a lot of non-Indian men, some with families, built shacks along the south end of this island and on past our village to April Point. April Point was called Poverty Point then because of the squatters. They fished with hand-lines from row boats and sold their catch to the scow that came around from the cannery at Quathiaski Cove. Almost all the way along on our reserve land there were squatters. That did not bother our people. Those were hard times for us, and we were all in it together. Times have changed. These little pieces of reserve land are all that we have left to us of all the territory that was ours. We always expected to be recognized as the rightful owners of the land that other people moved in on and took for their own. We are claiming this territory now. Indians signed no treaty here giving up our land and waters!

During the twenties I fished in summer and worked in a logging camp in the winter. The camp was International Logging in the mouth of the Campbell River. Our fellas worked on the booms. We had a boss named "Frenchie," who we got to know really well. We all got along fine. I remember those guys laughing with us and saying, "Okay, Go ahead. You guys must know what you're doing; you own this country!"

We all played in a baseball league together. Harry Moon was our team captain, and Frenchie was playing with us. We played other companies at Duncan Bay, Elk Bay branch of Marine Logging, and as far south as Courtenay and Nanaimo. We were high team, and in our fourth year we lost only one game. We had a great time.

During those tough years of the depression, I'd be working almost a year round. Every year we left Cape Mudge for Rivers Inlet in spring. I signed on first for Rivers Inlet in 1929. Our people all went off together as families around June twentieth on the Union Steamship that called at Quathiaski Cove twice a week. It was like a summer holiday beginning. It must have been like that in the old days when we had this country to ourselves and our people all started off together in spring from the winter village to head out to the summer camping grounds.

There were eleven canneries in Rivers Inlet. Tom Price of Cape

Mudge was a recruiter for Strathcona, and my father and Oscar Lewis hired the men for Wadhams. I worked for Wadhams for nine years. The company provided us with living quarters and little twenty-two to twenty-four-foot skiffs with sails. No motors were allowed in the inlet then, only sail. There had once been plenty of sockeye salmon in the inlet, but when the logging companies went in the fish went down. So to protect the fish no motors were used. The women worked in the canneries, and the men fished. We worked hard, and we had a very good time too. The best thing was that our friends and families were all there together. I remember that there was a big net-loft where we danced on the weekends. It was a lot of fun.

After spending the spring and early summer at Rivers Inlet, it was

ate 23
iffs with sails fishing in Rivers Inlet,
1905. Cheverton Album (8496
L)

time to return home to Cape Mudge. By August first we had move
again from Cape Mudge into the places provided for us by the canner
in Quathiaski Cove. We were fishing for the company in Area 1
Johnstone Strait from Deepwater Bay to Salmon River. The compan
had a lease on that area until around 1926 or 1927. After that we sti
fished in that area and didn't have any trouble with others coming in o
it, but we were not restricted any longer to that area and could fis
wherever we wanted.

Almost all the women at Cape Mudge worked in the cannery in th
Cove. The cannery stood where the big net loft is today. Some of th
houses for the workers are still there nearby. Ida and I and our fami
had a little cottage right on the stream by the ferry landing. The wome
fitted the fish into the cans. Chinese men slit, gutted, washed, and slice
the fish, and our women selected the slices that had to be put together i
one can and wrapped the fish to a tight fit with no gap at the centr
They liked the work. Later machines replaced some of the work of sli
ing the fish and making the cans, but no machine could replace the wor
native women did in the canneries. They became pretty expert at i
Some could do a fast and good job, and they made the most money b
cause they were paid by the number of cans they could fill.

Around the start of the last war, we fished for dog-fish (shark) righ
out here off our village. B.C. Packers was buying the fish from us. The
removed the livers for oil on a scow in Quathiaski Cove, and the rest
the fish went down to Vancouver to be filleted. I think they sent the fi
to England to feed the people or the troops. It was used in England f
"fish and chips" they say. Down in Vancouver, they had to quit the o
eration. The skin of the dog-fish is like sandpaper, and they could n
keep the saws in shape that were used to cut them up. I went out on th
vessels that were trawling for dog-fish. They used to lay a drag-net o
the bottom. The most we ever got in one day was ten to twelve tons

If you were above average in the fishing for the company for ten yea
you got to run a herring boat. After the fall salmon fishing, sometime
the 1940's, I'd be out for herring from November to Christmas and fro
mid-January to March. We were on an eighty-two-foot seiner betwe
here and Prince Rupert. When I think back on the stormy seas, how co
and tired we often were, I think its lucky I haven't got arthritis like
many of our people. For the last six years I fished I was only home to st
at Christmas time.

Long ago when I was a boy if the old people would see the sky clou
ing over in the late fall and early spring, they would say we'd^zulis, mea
ing white clouds. They knew the overcast sky had come to protect t

herring at spawning time. Well, that's a lot different than the way people look at the herring fishery today when you have to take all you can to make good in the fishing business.

We were out herring fishing and logging in the usual places in winter, then fishing for salmon at Rivers Inlet in spring, followed by summer fishing at Quathiaski Cove. Many of our people fished each fall off the Qualicum River. It wasn't my custom to fish down there. The company wanted me to go to Qualicum, but I didn't always go along with the company telling me where to fish. If a fight broke out, I'd tell them, "I'm quitting." Pretty soon they come around to say to me, "You can go where you want to." In my lifetime native people were still moving around with the seasons like they did in the days before other people ever came here. And we don't have to be told where the fish are! We are the experts on that!

In 1938, B.C. Packers Ltd. purchased the company from Anderson. Before the business was sold, we were called in and questioned on who we would be willing to work for. He said, "I'd like to see you people satisfied." My father wanted Bell-Irving because he knew him and had worked for him. Jimmy Hovell wanted Nelson Brothers. John Dick and I wanted B.C. Packers, and that's who Anderson sold out to. He told us then, "If I had sons to go into the business I would never sell out." We understood that. Anderson had three daughters.

In those early cannery days a lot of our people learned the trade language: Chinook. That was all that was spoken in dealings between Indian and non-Indian people. I could understand some, but I spoke Kwakwala and English. Compared to these languages, Chinook is simple. Very few non-Indians ever learned to speak Kwakwala. One man I knew for years in the fishing industry management spoke Kwakwala. Oh, he could speak it like a native! Only a few months ago I was down in his office in Steveston, and he was talking easily to me in our own language. That always surprised and pleased me. Then a guy from the Japanese people came into his office, and my friend said, "Excuse me," and started talking to him in his own language!

At first there were no radio intercoms on boats, but as soon as they were installed, there was a regulation put on so that we could not talk to each other in our own language. Alert Bay men sometimes use Kwakwala language on their boats, and I have told my sons to do the same. I tell my boys, "You use English and you might as well tell all the boats in this area where the fish are." Why not use our own language? The Yugoslavs and the Japanese use their own language. They don't want to tell the rest of the boats where they have found the fish! Why should

they? Sometimes today when a few of our boats are nearby, we use ou
own language, but mostly it's in English because that's what our skippe
speak most easily today.

When the intercoms were put on the boats, the company always trie
to find out from us where our guys were getting the fish so that the
could send other boats to fish there. I didn't want to tell them where th
fish were hitting. I was independent and didn't always go along wit
direction from the company. Once my son Don and I and Ed Chicki
were fishing off Nanaimo and took in sixteen thousand fish between u
I called in for the packer. "Where are you?" "Never mind," I said. "Yo
send the packer into Active Pass and we'll meet you there!"

There were times when the company told me to fish someplace, and
wouldn't go there because I knew the fish had gone through. One (
those times was when I was coming home to Cape Mudge after a week
fishing up around Alert Bay. I had a crew of five with me and it was ge
ting rough, so I tied up in Robson Bight. I just happened to check wit
the blue book and saw that in the year past on the same date the fis
were up around Addenbroke Light. So I left that night and went nort
It was slow going in the weather, but we reached Addenbroke aroun
eleven in the morning. Two boats were already there, and the men c
them called over to me and told me that I had just missed my bo
Steve, Mel, and Don and their cousin Bobby Clifton. The company ha
ordered the four boats further north into Whales Channel. After tha
the two boats pulled out, and we went 'round into the channel behin
Addenbroke Island. There were millions of fish, heading south for Rive
Inlet! Well, I told the crew we'll just go ahead and have our meal ar
wait for the fish to round a certain point of land. Then we hauled in fo
thousand salmon in four sets. The next day I got seven thousand fish
six sets, and we headed for the nearest packer at kʷakum (Kwakume I
let). After we offloaded, I took my boat into Namu for the night. There
got my boys on the phone and told them the fish were hitting at Adde
broke and to get on down to join me.

In those days Ross Nicholson in Vancouver held a conference at 8 p.r
with all the boats fishing for the company. The skipper on the pack
had tipped him off about the number of fish we had brought in, so h
got me on the phone and wanted to know where we got them. I didr
want to tell everybody on the boats where the fish were, so I said, "
the water." Oh, he got mad! "Pl-ease tell me where you got those fish
I told him at Addenbroke; and my records showed they would be ther
"Your record must be pretty good," he said.

We went out to Addenbroke again the next day, but there wasr much, so we headed home. On the way I got a call from Ross. He wanted to know why I left Addenbroke. I told him, and he asked me to call in at the office in Alert Bay. The product manager there called me into his office and ordered me back to Addenbroke. So I told him, "You want to own me *and* the boat! Well, you can't own me! You go ahead and take the boat! I'm not going back to Addenbroke." I knew that by this time the fish were down south heading for Johnstone Strait. He said, "What you going to do?" "I'm going to pull my net off. You want to run the boat, so take it! There are lots of other companies who want me to fish for them."

Well, Ross Nicholson flew in to Alert Bay from Vancouver, and he came down to the wharf and asked me to come up to the office. "What for? I don't like anyone that tries to run me! I'm the fisherman. He just sits in the office. He doesn't know what goes on on the water." So after a while with people going up and down between the wharf and the office, Ross came down and said to me, "I don't want to lose you. We're not going to bother you again. Go ahead and do what you like." So we fished down Johnstone Strait on the way home and brought in two thousand salmon to the packer at Knox Bay on the way.

We were always able to take care of ourselves. Indians don't join unions. I look at it this way. There is no help from the unions. If you are fired, the union cannot give you a job. It's the company that gave you the job. In the early days before I bought a boat of my own, I ran a company boat. In the company, if they thought you were a strong union man, they wouldn't have anything to do with you.

Native people and the people who managed the canneries worked pretty well together from the beginning. When the unions involved our people in a big strike up at Rivers Inlet around 1916, we lost out on our whole summer fishing season. What we lost out on was not just a job. Fishing is our living, our way of life! We own these waters, and we have to be able to fish them. That's why we have small reserves. Interior Indians have big land reserves. They need them for ranching and trapping. We need the sea for fishing.

After that strike our people got together at a big meeting at Alert Bay. My father and brother Dan went up, and an association for native fishermen was formed. My father and Dan went to all the villages in our area and on the West Coast and told our people how to protect themselves with their own association. Later, in 1936, we widened the membership to include seiners, gill-netters, and trollers. That was the Pacific Coast Native Fishermen's Association. It worked well for us. Then in 1938, Alfred Adams, Douglas Edenshaw, and Heber Clifton came down the

coast from the Charlottes forming the Native Brotherhood. When the
reached these parts, we turned over the money we held in the Fishe
men's Association and joined the Brotherhood. My father is still remen
bered all up and down the coast for his part in protecting the fishir
rights of our people. The Native Brotherhood is still strong in our are;

In 1929 we were going to strike right here at the cannery
Quathiaski Cove. Our Brotherhood representatives went with us to s￼
W. E. Anderson. We demanded a higher price for fish. We were real
surprised at his reaction. No questions asked. "If you guys want it, y￼
got it!"

August 1937 was the last great fishing season in the old cannery da￼
That year I brought in twelve thousand sockeye, sixteen thousand pink
and nine thousand chums to the cannery. In one lucky day I brought
forty thousand fish in two sets! I took my boat into Johnstone Strait ar
brought in twenty-five thousand fish in the first set: pinks, coho, ar
sockeye. After that set we went over to Green Sea Bay on Sonora Islar
and made a second set. From there we could see the salmon jumping ;
the way across the passage to Rock Bay on Vancouver Island. The cre
wanted to tie up to shore, but I said no. If we had tied up to shore, ￼
would have ended by having to dump four to five thousand fish becau;
there would be no room in the holds of our boat. We used half a net ar
pulled in another fifteen thousand.

At the cannery at Quathiaski Cove, they couldn't keep up with t￼
loads of fish coming in. The cannery would be working till elev￼
o'clock at night or later and starting up again at seven in the morning.
this particular year they were going from June to October. Spring, pir
sockeye, and chums were all heading down to the Fraser River. Fi
brought in to the cannery that could not be handled before the night w
through would be taken out into the middle of Discovery Passage ar
dumped; otherwise the fish went soft and were not fit for cannir
Sometimes ten to fifteen thousand fish were taken out and dumpe
There were so many fish that the cannery could not get the packers o
to where the boats were. We were told to take only one load a day. ￼
set once in the morning, fill my boat, and in an hour and a half be in
the cannery. Oh, there were a lot of fish of all kinds!

Fishing fell off after that, and in August 1941 when the cannery was
full swing, the whole operation was wiped out by fire. It happened
the early morning. When the watchman came along to blow the whist
he saw the fire and fainted. I was in my boat up in Johnstone Strait. T
cannery manager was on a boat nearby. I don't know how he knew abc
the fire because we had no telephones on our boats, but he came alor

side and told me, "Our cannery has burnt down."

There used to be a lot of fish, but what has been allowed to happen on the coast where we are has made the numbers go down. It is the logging that has ruined the fishing.

Before 1930 there was a regulation that prevented logging within half a mile of a salmon spawning stream. There have to be trees along a river bed, or it goes dry and the fish do not have the water they need. That's what happened to all the little creeks that went dead and to big rivers like the Oyster that are only now coming back to life. Now second-growth timber growing on the old cuts is beginning to hold the water in the gravel beds where the salmon spawn.

But now in the 80's the logging companies can take the trees right up

te 24
the B.C. Packers net loft, Quathiaski
ve. From left to right, Mel Assu (in
dow), with sons Perry and Douglas.
oto by John Gordon, 1985

to the stream bed. If they get a big price, like a thousand dollars a tree for fine cedars along the stream, they go right ahead and fall them. If there are only a few spawning salmon left or the price of fish is down, the Department of Fisheries and Oceans won't try to stop them.

Everyone realizes that fishing has been sacrificed for logging in British Columbia. Until this year when the stocks of fish are building up again it looked to us like our fishery was being wiped out.

In the summer of '85 there were around six hundred seine boats in all on this coast. Only one hundred of these would be run by native people. The number of our native people fishing in their own waters here on this coast has fallen off with the poor harvests and the restrictions on fishing. While our people lost out in many places, the number of non-Indian "fishermen" buying seiners on these waters built up. In my days as full-time fisherman, there were only about three hundred seiners, and the fish were here in great numbers as they had always been. Because too many boats have been chasing too few fish, some of our people who were fishing people here for thousands of years have been forced out of business.

Fisheries want the seine-boat fleet to be cut down, and I have been consulted by Fisheries on how to do it. A few years ago when Dr. Pearse was heading a commission to look into the whole matter of how to handle the fishing crisis on this coast, he phoned me and asked my opinion.[2] I told him that the fair way to cut down on the number of seine boats fishing is to take off the drum. If these seiners had to take off the drum, *real* fishermen could make a living in this business. But the "prairie farmers" and business investors would have to go. They would have to get out of the commercial fishing because they couldn't handle the job. When you are table-seining, you have to know what you are doing – what time to set your net, how to get it in when it's snagged, and all that.

Families fishing since 1925 know how to use the power block and tackle and could handle the table method. While I was in Japan recently they arranged for me to stay with a fishing family in a village where they drag-seine off the beach for needle fish. Over there, if a family is fishing they stay fishing. Nobody else can get in. That is the way I see it too. That is the right way. Indians would continue to fish here even if they took the drum off because our families know all the ways of fishing from the beginning. They are fishing people. People coming into the fishing business lately who are not real fishermen would be the ones to get out. If it wasn't for the drum, half the boats would be out of the fleet, and that's what's wanted. Anyone willing and able to handle the table

*…ate 25
…ne seiners at the centre are* Western
…ave, *owned by Don Assu, and*
…estern Eagle, *owned by Steve Assu.*
…e left is the* W9, *owned by Don Assu*
…d skippered by his son Brian. Photo*
…*Patrick Assu, 1980*

method could stay in.

Pearse said that there would be a problem because of the millions of dollars that have been invested in big modern seiners with drums. When our people move into big modern seiners with drums, we have a licence to run that new boat. It is transferred from whatever boat we owned before. We wonder where the businessmen who are investing their money in big seiners are getting their licences from. A new licence isn't legal. You have to get a licence from someone going out of the business. Legally there are no new licences. This is supposed to control the competition on the water for the limited number of fish. So where are the new licences issued by the federal government for big new seiners coming from?

I was the last to put a drum on my boat. I was fishing for B.C. Packers and they asked me why I was doing it. I was always better than average each year. I had to do that to get men to work for me! It's a lot easier with the drum. If they took off the drum, fewer fish would be taken. You can make twenty-five sets a day with the drum and only five with the table. Fishing with the drum is dangerous. Even with tons of ballast it is risky. Many boats have been lost and lots of men drowned since they put on the drum.

Once when I was out on my son Don's boat, the *Western Brave* – seventy-foot seiner – and we were going through Seymour Narrows at Ripple Rock, we slowed right down because it's really dangerous there. Behind us two boats were coming on at full speed, and when they hit the rip they shot clear across the channel. Lucky they didn't roll over – not much experience and in dangerous water, with boats top-heavy with drums. Repair bills for one boat salvaged after a roll-over in the narrows came to $100,000. Well, that's why marine insurance companies are going broke!

Just get rid of the drum, the radio, and the sonar if you want to know who the real fishermen are. Some of the latest gear for tracking fish doesn't seem right to me. The fish don't have a chance. The sonar that showed the schools of fish under the boat now lights up red or green tracking the fish as they move north or south under the boat. I went after the government to try to stop it. It makes me uneasy because the fair chance between the fish and our people that we always had in the old days is going forever. I'm against that.

Fisheries officers never used to listen to us. Now there seems to be a policy that they should consult us. They listen, but they don't hear. The department seems to bring in officers from the prairies. It doesn't make sense. They don't do anything about the serious situation the fishermen are in on this coast because they don't understand what's going on.

In 1984 when I was down at Willow Point, just south of Campbell River, a storekeeper showed me a truck loaded with fish in hot ice. He had been watching these guys bringing in one truckload of fish after another, and he wanted me to check on it. They were not sports-fishermen taking only a few per person because of the legal limit. They were taking all they could get their hands on, probably to sell in Vancouver. I phoned Fisheries in Campbell River. I told them what was happening and asked them to get down there quick. Their office is only a fifteen-minute drive from Willow Point. I waited there wondering why they never came. Finally, I phoned them back. They said that by the time they could have gotten there and back, it would have been after their office hours!

That's not the only time I have called Fisheries to help me control people breaking the law. A guy from Campbell River had set up a holding net for "herring" off our wharf at Cape Mudge. He was taking them across Discovery Passage to the wharf on the Campbell River side to sell to boaters or fishing resorts or whoever is buying herring bait for salmon. I went down and had a look at these fish. There were eight tons of young salmon. They were curling and flipping, and I knew all the kinds. I asked him, "Do you know what you have there?" "Herring," he said. "Listen here," I said. "Those are not herring; herring don't jump like that!" I was really mad. I told him: "You are breaking the law." He only said, "Oh, I didn't know." He knew.

My house is right above the wharf. I went straight there and phoned Fisheries. I asked them to stop him when he brought the next load of salmon fry into the wharf at Campbell River or to come across to our side and I would show them what was in the holding net. That man took five boatloads across to Campbell River. The next morning I phoned Fisheries. "Why didn't you get him when he came in on your side?" I asked. They had never even gone down to the wharf!

We all know about this; that's the way it is. Fisheries blames it on too few men on the job. They did a lot better in handling the fisheries when they had only one man on the job in my time!

Once when there was a lot of our boats up around Robson Bight waiting for the 6:30 A.M. time for setting our nets, we all saw this guy setting ahead of time. We decided to report him to Fisheries. In the afternoon we all went in to Port McNeill and phoned Fisheries. So, what happened? Nothing happened! Now when the Fisheries people come to me saying that some of our people are breaking the law, I remember those things. I tell them "That's your business, if someone is breaking the law, arrest them. Don't come to me!''

Nineteen eighty-five turned out to be the greatest fishing year in many years. For sockeye it was the best year since 1913. In the fall Johnstone Strait was a river of fish. There must have been five million chums running south to spawn. It was the first year in twelve years that we were permitted to take chum salmon. They were sweeping in from the cold waters of the North Pacific and moving down Queen Charlotte Strait, Johnstone Strait, and Discovery Passage. Out on the west coast of Vancouver Island, the fish rounded the southern tip and headed across the Strait of Georgia into the mouth of the Fraser River. It was a great year for fishing, but we were told we couldn't go out and fish!

While I was in Japan recently, the head of their Fisheries for Hokkaido Island was sitting next to me at dinner. He told me their people had tracked the salmon down the Pacific Coast to California and all the way back up to the Arctic where they make a big turn and head down the coast again to their spawning streams in Canadian waters. Before the fish head for California and are in international waters, the Japanese take them in huge factory ships. They run out lines for five miles, baited every two feet with hooks and bring in loaded lines with the salmon weighing two and a half to three and a half pounds. They put them up in tins right there on board ship. One reason for the big run of fish in our own local waters in 1985 was that the Japanese fishermen were on strike. Japan has had to move its fishing limit line back a hundred miles toward their own coast, and that helps preserve the salmon returning to their streams in Canadian waters.

The fish stocks here were building up, and we knew that 1985 was going to be a big one, but Fisheries kept the restrictions on fishing time for seiners to twenty-four hours in any one week or, at the most, forty-eight hours. In 1984, I wanted to prove to them that there was an increase in the numbers of all kinds of salmon passing through Johnstone Strait because we wanted to be allowed one additional twenty-four-hour period to take them. There were a lot of salmon. I took Fisheries officers out on my grandson Brian's boat – the *Western Monarch*. It was the end of the season; we were the last boat farthest south in Johnstone Strait. All other boats north of us had a chance to take the salmon before we did. I told Brian where to tie up and set, and we brought in two thousand fish of all kinds in two sets. Even that didn't convince the federal Fisheries people here that more fish could safely be taken by commercial fishermen without affecting the spawning.

Thousands more fish were passing under the boat in Johnstone Strait. They were heading for the Fraser River. There were too many salmon all ready entering the river! We told them that. Fisheries will call you in to consult: they ask your opinion – I don't know why, because you can't tell them anything.

In 1985, the Americans, who are restricted from taking too many sockeye returning by the southern route round Vancouver Island to their spawning grounds in Canada, have been taking our chums over the limit. These fall fish are covered by the treaty between our countries which limits the American take to a small proportion of the run. American gill-netters and seiners waited off Point Roberts, and when the tide went out sweeping the fish into U.S. waters, they scooped them up. Ninety thousand in one day! And while this was going on, we were tied up at the wharf! Canadians, refused the right to fish!

Up until the late 1930's I food-fished for our people in three villages, Cape Mudge, Campbell River, and Comox. It had been necessary ever since native people sold the catch they made each year to the company. So I'd bring in two or three thousand fish in a set and distribute them to all the families for their winter food. In the early forties I got the regulation on food-fishing changed so that families could go out and get their own fish twice a year. The regulation today makes it possible for any native fisherman to apply for a food-fishing permit, stating the number of fish required and for how many families. Fisheries boats are supposed to stand by. These fish for food have a fin and tip of nose cut off so they can't be sold – except illegally. We want this illegal sale stopped. We don't want the sale of food-fish made legal either. It would wipe out the fishery for honest fishermen, native and non-native alike.

Today native fishermen can apply for a cheaper licence for their boat; but with that restricted licence, only another native fisherman can buy the boat that uses that licence. But all Assu boats pay the full sixteen-hundred dollars to renew their annual licence so that they are not restricted. Our boats can incorporate as a business. It is of no advantage to the skipper/owner, but no income tax needs to be paid on the crew's wages because the business originates on the reserve. This helps the younger men coming on as crew to get started financially. We are negotiating with the government for a loan fund so that when our people are ready to get into the business they can buy a boat. It is hard for native people to get into this high-cost business today. Insurance on boats is high. And if there are not enough days opening to catch fish, you can lose your boat. It costs some of our seiners a thousand dollars a day just to be tied up at the wharf.

Because we are prevented from taking the salmon, there is a terrible waste of the fish. On the Skeena, the Fisheries made a mistake and as usual underestimated the number of sockeye that could be taken in 1985. Thousands of fish died trying to enter the river to spawn. The fishermen knew they were there because they are the experts, but the Fisheries thought they knew better. Now it is the same up Rivers Inlet, Bute Inlet, Loughborough Inlet; the salmon returned to spawn in their millions, but we were prevented from taking them. By taking these fish we would have stopped the second run from digging out the eggs of fish that had already gone upriver and spawned. There were too many fish up the rivers already.

Here in Johnstone Strait they closed the fishing the first week in September when the pinks had gone through. Then they permitted only one day after that, on October 7th, for just twenty-four hours for chums. In area twelve and thirteen – Alert Bay to the southern end of Johnstone Strait – 381,000 fish were taken by four hundred boats on that one-day opening. It should have been plain proof to Fisheries that a great run of fish was underway, but they kept on with closure.

Over at Nitinat on the west coast of Vancouver Island an opening was allowed for one day extra. Fisheries figured on a surplus of a hundred thousand fish. The fishermen took in over a million fish on that one day. There was no problem for the canneries. Most of the catch was sent up to the Prince Rupert canneries. Any chum salmon brought down to Fraser were just iced up and shipped to Japan.

Our biggest problem is getting enough time on the water to make a living fishing. We have only twenty-four hours a week for seining: and at best we may get two days a week; yet the cost of this business has shot up high.

Even when we know that a great number of fish are passing through Johnstone Strait, we can't get Fisheries to understand that. They refuse to grant another day opening or an extension of the season.

I know what is happening in the sea. I know how many salmon are moving down to the Fraser River to spawn and how many we can take without affecting a good spawning. I know because I have a lifetime of experience on the water and the experience of my people before me. In 1984 I went to Fisheries to tell them that there were a million salmon between our area and the Fraser River, so we should have a few more days fishing here while the fish are in good condition and bring the best price. The Fisheries officer said to me, "Oh, is that what you think?" "No!" I answered. "That's not what I think, that's what I know."

We have the Native Brotherhood to take up problems like this for us. They negotiate the price we receive for our fish with the companies every year. The Native Brotherhood works out the price with the United

Fishermen and Allied Worker's Union, but we are independent. The Native Brotherhood has meant everything to the Indians. We get together in convention every year and handle our legal problems and anything else that comes up. That's where we plan for the future. During the fishing season the officers of the Native Brotherhood are out fishing, so sometimes we have to take direct action ourselves until we can bring it to the meeting; then they back us up.

The Native Brotherhood is as active here now as it used to be farther north along the coast. The numbers of boats owned or operated by native fishermen in our area has built up in recent years, and we are all Native Brotherhood here. Most of our boats used to be gill-nets, but after the 1940's more seiners came into use. We'd be changing over during the season, with the gill-netters going north to Rivers Inlet in June, and when they returned in August, a shift over was made to the seiners.

In the old times, the fishing grounds for our people was the Queen Charlotte Strait and Johnstone Strait region and other areas nearby. For the Lekwiltok (our tribe including Cape Mudge) the fishing area was on Johnstone Strait and on the Mainland opposite. We fish mainly today in Johnstone Strait. It's almost entirely seiners now, and seiners can't fish farther south in the Strait of Georgia.

Each family with boats at Cape Mudge and Campbell River has their own place for fishing in Johnstone Strait, and the others understand that. It works like this today; the seven seiners of the Assu family start at Green Sea Bay and fish to Little Bear River. The four Lewis seiners hang around above Little Bear River at Ripple Point. Above that the Roberts family run their six seiners. The four Quocksister seiners are far up around Camp Point below Salmon River. The Dicks have two seiners and stay just below Pineapple Point south of Bear River. The Price family run two seiners, the Billy family run two seiners, and the Chickite family three seiners – all in fishing places around Green Sea Bay. The Chickite family also have two gill-netters. The Greys have a troller longliner. The gill-netters and trollers fish up around Deepwater Bay, but they can move anywhere in Johnstone Strait or the Strait of Georgia.

A lot of families own aluminum punts with motors for roe-herring fishing. There are very big runs of herring out on the west coast in spring when they come in a path a mile wide and ten to twelve miles long. Some years Fisheries decide to close the herring fishery on the west coast altogether. No openings for us to fish!

The world market for fish has been good. The economy on this coast has been very bad. Our towns rely on the commercial fishermen. If they have a bad year, the retail stores suffer because they are the ones who

Plate 26
Fishing imagery in stained glass.
Window in the Quadra Island United
Church. Commissioned by Ruby
Wilson in honour of her parents, Louise
and James Hovell. Photo by Bob
Plecus, 1985

supply the fleet. Prosperous fishermen ensure a prosperous economy. Some people say that federal Fisheries just doesn't understand regional problems, and we would be better off under the provincial government. But the provincial government is more anxious for the success of the sports fishery because of tourism than they are for the livelihood of local fishing people. Fish farms are being encouraged (newcomers, some of them bringing in Atlantic salmon which are subject to various diseases) instead of solving the basic problems of the fishing people. You can't solve basic problems by encouraging competition in the market for fish.

In 1985, in a last try to show Fisheries that there were millions of fish going through Johnstone Strait on their way to spawn, my son Mel took the guys from Fisheries, Safeway Ltd., and United Fisherman's and Allied Workers Union out into Johnstone Strait to make a test set. We brought in three thousand fish. It was blowing so hard that we had to make a set where we could and not where the fish were. I estimate that five million fish went through the passage then. The take could have been much larger if we could have gone where they were. We were refused another twenty-four hours' fishing, and the season closed.

So, our women went to the Fisheries office to protest. At first no one would speak to them. They went there to demand a day's opening. They know that the Fisheries make these test sets in a pattern and that the fish don't run in these patterns. You have to be a fisherman on the water fishing to know where the fish are running.

I called in at the Fisheries office because I had a meeting there. I was really surprised to see the women crowded into the office; some were even sitting on the floor. My own daughter, my daughter-in-law, and the wife of my grandson were there! When Fisheries officers finally agreed to meet with them, their demand for another day fishing was refused. I figure seiners on this coast lost $2.5 million in the best season ever since 1937 because of Fisheries bungling. We lost out, the whole community lost out, while the fish died by the thousands at the river mouths.

The last opening of the season was November 25th farther south at the mouth of the Qualicum River on Vancouver Island. By the time that catch was taken the fish were rotting, and B.C. Packers refused to pack the garbage.

It is hard to see into the future for our people. Some people say that we should go the same way as native people in Washington State where half the catch is guaranteed to them by law. If they don't get 50 per cent of the catch, they can use their own methods like weirs to bring in their share.[3] But here the native share of the catch is not the problem. We do well in the industry. What we are struggling with are those things that affect the whole industry: buying back boats to reduce the fleet, stopping the issuing of new licences, protesting the setting up of fish farms. The regulation governing our time for fishing in these waters doesn't make sense because the Fisheries don't know what's going on out there and can't control it anyway. I told them so at a big meeting here with Fisheries where all commercial fishermen were protesting. I told them, "You should all be fired!"

There will have to be altogether new directions to get us out of this situation. We have to look to the future possibilities. Perhaps flying in fresh fish to the early morning fish market in Tokyo where nearly a million people gather every day to buy. It would bring the highest prices for the finest quality fish. We have to take new directions. That's the way it has always been for our people here at Cape Mudge.

6
Life in the Village of Cape Mudge

We have had a Christian congregation meeting at Cape Mudge village since the missionary teacher came in 1878. We are the only village of the Lekwiltok tribe of the Kwagiulth Nation to build a church. People in the other Lekwiltok villages at Salmon River near Kelsey Bay, at Campbell River, and at Comox met together in their own villages when the minister from Cape Mudge called there, but they came here for baptism, weddings, and funerals, just like they often do today. Each village had its own cemetery. We put one in here at Cape Mudge in 1891. In the late 1930's the remains from the old Indian burial houses were brought in, and I arranged for the cement crosses to mark the graves. John Dick Sr. kept track of births, deaths, and marriages, but the records have been lost.

Some people say that Christianity is not the tradition of our people. Well, we've been Christian for over a hundred years now.

The church meant an awful lot to us in those early days. Everybody helped out and everybody attended the services. We worked for the church, but we had our own beliefs, and we carried on with our custom of dancing and potlatch. At Cape Mudge there was never any trouble over this that I heard about.

By the time that I was born in 1905, there was an act on the books making it against the law for Indians to carry on their dances and the potlatch; and a few people from different coastal tribes were sent down to court in Vancouver for potlatching, but I don't think anything much came of it, at least not until later in 1922 when the government began arresting our people here. At Cape Mudge when I was growing up, we invited our ministers to the potlatches, and they came and enjoyed themselves.

My father built an old-style big house in 1910 for potlatch. That wa
eighteen years after the Methodist Mission was here. In 1911 he gav
the biggest potlatch that was ever given at Cape Mudge at the time I wa
growing up. His potlatch was followed by those of other leading men
and these big potlatches calling in all the fourteen tribes of th
Kwagiulth were not over till around 1917. When I look back now, I wisl
they had saved my father's house, but people didn't feel that way then

When we built a modern village here at Cape Mudge in the 1920's
each family had a new-style house of their own, and the last of the bi
houses came down, and only a few posts or poles were left. There wer
no big potlatches here for over fifty years, but some potlatching went o
just in peoples' families. High-ranking people were sometimes called t
potlatches in other villages, but mostly potlatching was over every
where.

This is the way of the Methodist Mission came to Cape Mudge. Th
mission ship *Thomas Crosby* used to put in at the villages in this area
and our people wanted a teacher and a school, so my father went aboar
the *Crosby* and asked for a missionary to be sent here to teach an
preach. He hinted that if this didn't happen fairly soon he might have t
go elsewhere!

In those days the Anglicans, Methodists, and Catholics really hate
each other, though they seemed to be doing the same thing. The Roma
Catholics really wanted to come in here. They were already in the vil
lages on the Mainland opposite. My grandfather told me that the peopl
of Church House once arrived in canoes bringing a Roman Catholi
priest, but our people wouldn't let them land. They pushed the canoe
out into the Pass. That wasn't very nice, but I understand how they fel
about it. Even today, people are coming down here and going door t
door *still* trying to convert us to Christianity and get us to come to thei
meetings. We chose the Methodist Church before 1892, and we hav
our own church we built ourselves fifty-four years ago. We already hav
a minister of the United Church here who was asked to call on th
people in their houses. These others come here and sit in my house
They make me very angry. Berta Billy, a member of our board of stew
ards, has said: "It's like trying to steal fish out of somebody else's boat.'

The Methodist Mission sent a permanent teacher to live at Cap
Mudge, and in 1892 R. J. Walker arrived with his family. We set asid
2.3 acres for the Mission. The Walkers stayed until 1904 and the
moved over to Gowlland Harbour on this island, but they kept in touc
with our people.

We didn't want a single man as a missionary. We had had single me

Plate 27
*R. J. Walker, the first teacher sent to
Cape Mudge by the Methodist
Missionary Society in 1892, at a
reunion held in his honour at Cape
Mudge in 1953. (BCAA)*

come and stay only a year or so and leave. Even before that, Rev. A. J. Hall of the Church of England at Fort Rupert had called in with William Broachie, but they were set up at Fort Rupert – too far away.

We built a house of milled lumber for the Walkers and had it ready when they came. Then Mr. Walker and the men of the village built the school. It was where the nursery school is now. It was only a one-room school, nothing fancy, but it was our chance to learn. Children were taught arithmetic, spelling, and English. Older people in the village came to the school to learn. At first Mr. Walker didn't speak Kwakwala. He spoke English in the school, and we soon got on to it. We could speak our own language in the playground or anywhere else. There was no problem about it like there was up at Alert Bay, where they thought Indians could only learn English if they forgot their own language.

Having a school at Cape Mudge meant the children didn't have to leave home and go away to school at Alert Bay. A few from around here had to go there because of problems in the family. My wife Ida's father died when she was four, and her mother died when she was seven, so she went to that home-school. Lucky for her; she really liked it.

At first the church services were held in the school. Mr. Walker preached in Chinook. He taught belief in God and Jesus Christ. We had

printed hymnbooks in Chinook and in Kwakwala. There were picnics and Christmas presents and Sunday School, and later on there was hymn-singing. The missionaries taught about the Holy Land and stories from the Bible. We still have a magic lantern and slides in our church that must have been used to show these things. Mr. Walker and his wife worked hard for the church here. They were always helping the people.

The Methodists were against strong drink and gambling. They wanted to keep people from trying to break up marriages, and they tried to stop the prostitution of Indian women in the logging camps around here.

We had our own marriage customs. As far as I know, we never had alcohol or prostitution before the white people came, and we didn't play lahal, our coastal Indian gambling game, here at Cape Mudge. Anyway, it is really a game of tricking the opposing team. The bets are very small. The Indians of Chemainus used to play it when they camped on the reserve here while they fished for the cannery at Quathiaski Cove. A few came over from the Campbell River band to join them, but no one went from here so far as I know. There was a lot of gambling in the lumber camps.

Our big problem was bootleggers selling liquor to our people. We were always trying to keep them out of the villages. I have heard that my father and Mr. Walker used to patrol the beach off our village at night when they learned that ships from San Francisco were on their way up here selling whiskey. It was in little bottles, and it must have been terrible stuff because it drove people crazy.

When the *Cottage City* was wrecked off Cape Mudge at the southern tip of our island in 1911, it was around Christmas time, and there was food and liquor on board for all the logging camps and places up north of here. Everybody was carrying off the cargo. The police were trying to locate the stuff, especially the liquor. Jim Smith and Francis Drake at Campbell River and Tom Price and my father at Cape Mudge were deputized and made responsible for their villages. They tried to keep the whiskey out.

At one time Indians in B.C. couldn't bring liquor on to the reserves. They had to drink it in beer parlours. It was only later that the law became the same for all people. Then each band voted on its own as to whether they wanted liquor on the reserve. In 1963 Cape Mudge voted "dry." Some people here today drink liquor, but we don't have any big problem with alcohol. It's just like anywhere else. We worked hard in the church for that!

By the time I was ready to go to school, Mr. Rendle had taken over from Mr. Walker. He stayed the longest of any teacher at Cape Mudge.

Plate 29
The United Church at Cape Mudge
after its 1979 restoration. Rev. Daniel
Bogert-O'Brien with members of the
board of stewards, Mary Billy at left
and Harry Assu and Pauline Dowler
at right. Photo by Hilary Stewart, 1985

from 1904 to 1918. We liked him, and I liked school. There were around twenty of us. We behaved in school. We wanted to learn. Oh, that Mr. Rendle was a busy man! He called in on the people in all our villages and the logging camps and was visiting the sick and getting them out to hospital. I used to run his open boat for him, and we were always on the go.

After Mr. Rendle, we had some ministers who didn't stay very long. Later on two native ministers served here. Rev. Peter Kelly was stationed at Nanaimo, but he came here whenever he was needed. He would bicycle the hundred miles up Vancouver Island from Nanaimo, cross by boat to our island, and then return home the same way. The Rev. Bill Robinson was with us here for a while and still calls in on us.

The Methodist Church joined in to form the United Church in 1925. Six years later we built our church. We named the church Walker Memorial for our first missionary teacher. Rev. Knox was here then. John Dick Sr. was the head carpenter and did all the finishing of windows, pews, and altar. All the men of the village pitched in and helped. We raised $2,200 to build the church. It was a lot of money in those days. My father and John Dick Sr. each gave $200.

The women of the village had been meeting together with Mrs. Knox, and they raised money for the building fund. They got a women's association started in 1929, and it was the first time that women had got together. Men had pretty much handled things before that, just like they do everywhere else I guess. Some certificates were given to the women in 1962 for thirty years of service to the church: Mrs. Billy Assu, Mrs. Oscar Lewis, Mrs. Jack Naknakim, and my wife, Ida Assu.

The women's club has kept going all these years. Today they call themselves the Cape Mudge Community Club, and they still put on the Christmas party for the children in the church, and every year they prepare the salmon barbeque to raise funds for the church. They have bought the equipment for the adventure playground for the village, and they help out with whatever is going on, especially for the children.

Well, back in 1932 we opened our church on April 24th. It was Easter Sunday. We had ordered a big brass bell from Vancouver for eighty dollars, and when the bell rang out that morning, we were all very proud of our church.

We have had twenty-four ministers at Cape Mudge. We've been pretty lucky in the men who came here. Ministers who mixed the most were the ones that built up the congregation and got things moving. I was always strong on having the minister visit our people in their homes.

Mostly it has been that way, but about forty years ago I found something out about the attitude of the church to my people that I have never forgotten. We had a young minister here at the time, Rev. T. T. Moore, and he was getting along fine. My father had requested that a younger man be sent up, and since Moore was just graduating from college the church sent him.

Jimmy Hovell and I went down to the B.C. Conference of the United Church in Vancouver with Rev. Moore, and there he got in trouble with the rest of the ministers. I knew them all. They said he was mixing too freely with our people! That was the first time I knew that ministers were told how our people were to be treated. They were mad at Moore because he had not done what he'd been told. They told him to see people in the manse or, if he called at the homes, to stay on the porch or, if he had to go inside, he was to leave the door open. He spoke up and told them: "I eat with them and I sleep with them!" After the Conference, he left Canada for the States and never came back. I have never attended another Conference, but I have remained with the church, and I am an elder. So while the church has been good, it has been up and down with the times.

A big change took place in our congregation in 1979. That was the year the band voted to open up the church to anyone on the island wanting to attend. Until then the church had been a mission to Indians. Since

Plate 30
Rev. Ron Atkinson serves fish at communion to Sandy Billy. Harry Assu, in the background, serves the bread. Photo by Mitch Hirano, 1980. Courtesy Dan Billy

Plate 31
Carved east wall (reredos) in the
church at Cape Mudge. The work was
commissioned from Haida artist Bill
Reid and carved by Jim Hart. Photo by
John Gordon, 1985

then the congregation, the board of stewards, and even the elders come from anywhere on the island. It works out really well. In 1979 we renamed the church "Quadra Island United Church" so everyone would understand that it was open to everyone.

Rev. Ron Atkinson came back at that time to Cape Mudge, and we started a project to restore the old building. It was in pretty bad shape. We all worked together on that, and the B.C. Heritage Trust and the Vancouver Foundation helped with supplies and skilled labour. Finally, the church was carpeted and the outside painted white. It really stands out at the centre of the village. You can see it from offshore with the bell-tower pointing to the sky. The building is now a heritage site.

We already had cross and candles, offering plates, and baptismal font, but because everybody was coming together in what had been a church for native people, it was decided that we should buy a few things made by Indian people. It didn't have to be by Kwagiulth carvers only. We wanted to open up. The church was everywhere on this coast, not just here.

Ruby Wilson gave a window in remembrance of her parents, James and Louise Hovell. It shows a fish boat with a mast like the cross. It's really nice. Russ Fuoco made it, and he made glass lantern lights for the sanctuary.

A button-blanket altar cloth with the Tree-of-life on it was planned by Dora Cook and sewn by my daughter-in-law Louisa with the help of other women in the village. In June 1980 it was dedicated in the church. The pearl shell buttons on the altar cloth came from United Churches all across Canada. Some buttons even came from Hawaii.

We serve bread, fish, and wine for communion, and that's when the elders wear their button-blankets. Communion is our most important ceremony. We have served fish with the bread and wine for six years now because fish was the food of our people. Cedar branches are brought in and put by the wall behind the altar. Cedar was important to our people. Almost everything we had was made from cedar.

In 1981 we asked Bill Reid, the Haida artist, to carve the east wall. He came up and sat in the church for a long time deciding how to handle it. He drew two big salmon swimming in a circle and got Jim Hart on the job to work it out on cedar boards and carve the wall. It took us time to find the yellow cedar boards that Bill would work on. Finally Walter Koerner got the right log for us, and he and Steve Assu paid for the boards.

The fish design was chosen because it is the sign of the Christian. To me it means a lot because in the early days our people depended for life

on the salmon. Our villages were always near the rivers where the fis
returned in the fall after they've spent their life in the sea. The fis
means an awful lot to us. It is really nice the way the native and nor
native way of life fits together in our church. We are not so narrow
minded any more. People learn from each other.

When the wall was put in, in April 1984, we had a service in th
church, and Jim Hart came up to be with us. Bill Reid was in New Yor
and couldn't come. On that day we held a procession from the church t
the beach where we put on the First Salmon Ceremony. I hadn't see
that done in our village for seventy years. Everyone tasted the first fou
salmon of the season, and then twins carried their bones back into th
sea. Our people think of twins as salmon people. Mabel and Emma, Jir
Sewid's twin daughters, were brought into shore by boat and give
bones in a new cedar bark mat. Then they went offshore a little way an
sunk the bones in the sea. This ceremony shows respect for salmon.

In our church we have silk-screen prints by Tony Hunt and Tim Pau
Mary Billy gave the Tony Hunt print in memory of her husband Sand;
It is in Kwagiulth style and represents the baptism of Jesus. The Tir
Paul print is in West Coast style. He is from the Hesquiat band. His sill
screen print shows Christ as Raven. The church has other works by na

Plate 32
Bobby Joseph, drumstick raised, calls a
farewell in Kwakwala to the Sewid
twins Mabel and Emma, who have
taken the remains of the first salmon
out to sea before sinking them
ceremoniously. James Wilson is at the
centre. Photo by Hilary Stewart, 1984

tive artists. Ernie Henderson, a carver from Campbell River, was commissioned to carve a full-size adzed cedar cross. It was dedicated on a Good Friday morning when it was set up outside in front of the church.

There is really good music in our church. Lots of our members are musicians. They sing and play for concerts to raise money for the church. A good organ was given to us for our use by Margaret Large. She is the grand-daughter of Richard Large, who was the Methodist missionary doctor at Bella Bella. We have really good people to play for our services.

We have shown that we respect the life of different people in our church. So far as our Kwagiulth people are concerned, we have had singing and prayers in Kwakwala by our members, but as the years go by, very few attending the church speak the language. For me what is important is that people from two communities have got to know each other, to be friends and respect each other. Our ministers have gone over to the Kwagiulth Museum to give the blessing of the church on our Kwagiulth customs. But people go to the museum when they want to learn about native customs. We do things different here from back-east Indians; even different from the Indians who live nearest to us in the Interior. We didn't have many really public events like the First Salmon Ceremony that I know of. Our Kwagiulth ceremonies are owned by families. You have to own them in order to have the right to show them, and they are to be shown in the potlatch.

Another good minister is with us now, Rev. Dan Bogert-O'Brien. I like him. He's easy to get along with. The services are good. He started morning service especially for families. He's doing a lot of good work for the sick at home and in the hospital, and I see him visiting in the houses with the people here at Cape Mudge and being with the men on the wharf and where they are roasting fish. To me, that's what he should be doing. That's what we invited him here to do.

Nowadays there are fewer of our people coming to church regularly, but many still come for baptisms, marriage, and funerals like they always used to do, and some who don't attend give money to keep the church going. Whenever I travel to a village or even to the city, I think the church is the backbone of the community. You are taken to the church as a baby for baptism, you are married there with all the people, and that is where you are taken when you die. It is the centre.

We got our start on education through the church school on the reserve here and in the home-schools run by the churches in Port Alberni, Chilliwack, and Alert Bay. The trouble was that Indians were only allowed to go to grade nine, and then they had to get out. A man who

came here once told me the missionaries didn't want us to have muc
education, but I don't know about that. I wanted my boys to go to hig
school, so I went to see the Indian agent, M. S. Todd, and told him so
He said to me, "Nothing doing!" I asked him, "Isn't it for everybody?
and he answered me, "Not for you people." We were really treated rot
ten in those days. It has pretty well changed now.

When I got home I was very angry, and I went straight to Rev. Moor
and told him how the agent had said, "You're lucky to get publi
school!" Rev. Moore said, "We'll go tomorrow to see the head of th
school district." So we went and talked to this man for a while, and
told him what the agent has said to me: "If an Indian student is sixtee
years of age, he's out!" I asked the school administrator, "Can I get m
kids into high school?" He said "Sure. But we'll have to by-pass the In
dian Affairs Department. Could you pay $125 each. Yes? Then sen
your boys to Heriot Bay High School on Monday morning."

So two of my boys were the first here at Cape Mudge to get a hig
school education. Rev. Moore coached them at nights, and they got o
well in their work. Later in the same year, I attended a Liberal part
meeting in Courtenay, and a young man came over to sit by me. He wa
the first lawyer in Campbell River. He asked me what had happene
over getting a high school education for my sons. I told him about th
struggle I had had to get those boys into high school. Luckily, the Liber
party representative was leaving for Ottawa right away, and he was tol
about it by the lawyer, and about three weeks later word came back tha
native kids could attend any public high school. That is when it opene
up for our people.

That fall my boys went down to King Ed in Vancouver to finish the
high school. They were the first native Indians to attend that school. Th
principal there, Mr. Wilson, welcomed us. He told us that they had stu
dents from every other ethnic group in Vancouver, and he had bee
looking forward to having some of our people. He said, "Kids here don
make any difference between races. They are all one here."

Now our people can pretty well attend any school, college, or unive
sity of their choice. My grandsons have attended a private school fc
boys on Shawnigan Lake. People didn't think education was so impo
tant for girls in the early days, but we sent our youngest girl to Pitman
Business College.

In the 1960's when the Evans were serving the church here, m
daughter-in-law, Cissy Assu, helped Mrs. Evans get the nursery schoo
going for kids. After Mrs. Evans left, Cissy volunteered to keep th
school going, and she kept it going for another year. It is still going.

A lot of young people from Cape Mudge have a high school education now, and some have university. They are trained in teaching, social service, secretarial work, government, law, business, museum work, and nursing. When visitors come here to Cape Mudge and say how "lucky" we are to have so many able people in this band, I am thinking to myself, "Well, we are not all that 'lucky' you know! Our people went ahead by standing up for our rights."

When we were kids we would play at potlatching. We'd call out names and hand out stuff and drum and sing. We weren't playing cowboys and Indians here, you know!

We used to play a game on the beach with a kelp bulb for a head. We cut eyes, nose, and mouth in the bulb and buried it in the sand. The others had to guess where it was hidden, and when it was found, we threw spears at it. The spears stuck in because we had made tips out of the wire of a lard pail handle.

Some men in each village were known for their great strength. They were the leaders in our games. The strong man in our village was nold^{z}e. That means "Big Fear." We called him Dr. Powell. He is buried in the graveyard here at Cape Mudge. He died in the cold walking home to our village on the old horse road that ran here from the south end of the Island. It was night, and he never made it. He used to drink quite a bit, and one time when he was put in jail at Comox for being drunk, he twisted the iron bar off the door of the place and escaped.

Dr. Powell was a champion at pole-vaulting, and he was the strong man on our team when we played Indian rugby. He was our goalie, and he sat at the end of the field on a hole just big enough to put the ball in. A side of six men threw the ball to each other and fought their way down the field and finally yanked the goalie off the hole and drove in the ball. I was around ten years old when I saw it played, and everybody was laughing and cheering on the team. I still laugh when I think about it.

The fastest runner of our people was Johnny Ferrie from Campbell River. Oh, how he could run! Around the spring of 1919, he won every race at the sports day at Cumberland: the 100 yards, the 220, the mile, and the five-mile. He used to drink a clamshell full of some root pounded in water on the day before the race. He'd be throwing up in only a minute or two, but on the next day when the races were held, he said he felt so light he could fly. Our men used to beat their legs with needle branches and rub them down with a plant softened in water. I don't know what the plant was.

Sandy Billy was the fastest runner at Cape Mudge. When Sandy was born, Johnny Ferrie took his birth cord and ran with it with all his might.

They say that that was the way Sandy got the power to be a runner.

We used to play organized games like baseball and soccer here at Cape Mudge. Around 1921 I started to play baseball with our team and played for nine seasons. Jimmy Wallace organized our team and league games. We played Campbell River, Courtenay, Cumberland, Union Bay, Comox, and the Indians at Powell River. Harry Moon, son of the chief at Salmon River, lived at Cape Mudge then, and he was a really good pitcher. He'd get us up in the early morning to practise, and one year he started the practice in January. We lost only one game that year.

Around 1924 the Church House people held a sports day on the spit on the Campbell River, and they wanted us to make up a team to play against them in a game of soccer. We didn't know anything about this game, but Jim Smith and a couple of others said they had played it, and so we decided to play against the Church House team. They told us how to play, where to stand on the field, all that, and we played them and beat them! It was a lot of fun.

After that we played soccer here at Cape Mudge. Dave Moon coached us, and after a while I became captain. We played in a league with nearby villages. The O. B. Allen cup had been held by Courtenay for five years, but when our team got some fine young players and really got

Plate 34
Tyee Soccer Team. From left, standing: Dave Moon, manager; Don Assu, Ivan Dick, S. Marshall, Albert Wilson, James Wilson, Steve Assu, Walter Billy, Herb Assu, Sandy Billy, and Harry Assu, coach. Seated, from left: Dan Billy, Elmer Dick, Mel Assu, Skip McDonald, goalie; William Dick, Jack Naknakim, and Wesley Dick. Courtesy Dan Billy

going, we brought that cup home to Cape Mudge. We played right up to the 1950's.

It was a lot of fun. We don't have these games in the village today. The best of the players grew older, and nobody was coming on. Young men seem to have other things to do in these days. So far as sports are concerned, there is nothing at Cape Mudge. It was good when we worked hard and played hard like that.

In the early days when my father was held responsible for the people here at Cape Mudge, he had to be always on the watch for the authorities trying to pull off some deal. When I took over from my father in 1954, I still had to be watching out for the kind of thing that could happen. You don't forget how they tried to keep control on us.

Around 1917–1919, William Halliday was Indian agent for this region. He wanted to get a contract for Wilson and Brady to log twenty million board feet of timber off our reserve here at Cape Mudge. They were the outfit with the railroad running from the south end of this island to their log dump on our reserve at Drew Harbour. We decided that we would handle it for ourselves: Assu, Dick, Hovell, and Wilson. Pretty soon Wilson and Brady heard about it, and they came round and offered my father a bribe of five thousand dollars to talk our people into letting them handle the job. My father refused and informed Halliday that Wilson and Brady would not get the contract.

Perhaps that bribe of five thousand dollars looked good to Halliday. While we were away fishing up at Rivers Inlet, he came down here to Cape Mudge and tried to get signatures on the Wilson and Brady contract from the few people left in the village. He got eleven "X's" and one signature. Too bad that man learned how to write! When we came in from Rivers Inlet by boat, all the timber was gone off our reserve, and Wilson and Brady had just pulled out.

It was in the 1950's that for the first time bands could run elections to choose their chief. The people could elect councillors according to the number in the band: one representative for each one hundred members. The terms were for two years. I was elected chief councillor in the first eight elections and served for sixteen years. Sandy Billy and Mary Lewis were elected to the first council with me. People liked them. Mary was a nice quiet woman. I remember our men smiling and saying, "Well, we're going to see how it works out." Mary worked out fine, but that was the only time we ever had a woman on the band council. By 1959 advanced bands running their own affairs could arrange for a band manager. My son Don was made band manager in 1959 and has worked with the council ever since.

When I was in office, there was the problem of our elected officers trying to make decisions and carry them out while the government agents were still trying to run things to their own advantage. I began to spend more and more time away from the village, what with the herring fishery opening up. So, I nominated Lawrence Lewis as the next chief councillor, and he was elected. He asked me: "Why me?" I told him, "You're in the village more than I can be and you can keep control better over our own business." Sure enough, he started running into the same kind of problems I had had. He was a good chief councillor and worked hard to stay ahead of the game. Of course things have changed a lot since my days on the council, but sometimes Ottawa treats us just like they did a hundred years ago. While Lawrence Lewis was chief councillor, we put up a plan to become a municipality at Cape Mudge so that we could be independent and handle all our own affairs. I was all for it, but a few people here went all around the village telling the people not to vote for it, and in the end the whole plan was lost by a few votes.

Everything important to our people at Cape Mudge and Quinsam is discussed at band meetings at Cape Mudge. All planning and everything that's to do with fishing or our community is talked over by those elected to band council. That's where decisions are made. If the people have any problem to discuss, they come here. Everything to do with our public campsite on our reserve at Drew Harbour is handled from the band office, also logging on any of our reserves and leases for lighthouse and gravel pits. People from Indian Affairs, police, schools and others are in and out. It's really busy. We have to arrange for a lot of important people and groups coming through all the time to see what we have been able to do here.

Two big problems are up to the band council now. One is the old issue over Quinsam Reserve. Our band owns it, but the Campbell River band claims it. Our two bands should be working together, not fighting each other. We would have a lot more strength if we were working together. I have even favoured amalgamation of our two bands, but with the way things have been going lately there doesn't seem to be much chance of that!

The new issue we have to face is how to handle all the people who apply to come back to live on the reserve now that the federal government changed the Indian Act with Bill C-31 (1985). There will be a lot more "legal Indians" than have been on the government list up till now. Indian men who took their share of band funds and pulled out of Cape Mudge to live somewhere else (franchised) can come back now to live

Plate 35
Louise Hovell of Cape Mudge, with Prime Minister Pierre Elliott Trudeau and Margaret Trudeau, on the occasion of an informal visit to Cape Mudge. 1972. Photo courtesy Ruby Wilson

here with their families. Most of them live outside where they wanted to be, but a few will come back.

A lot more people will be band members now that women who married non-Indians are applying for legal status. When that is granted, these women are automatically band members; their children too. Lots of women who married-out are coming back to live, and they are building houses here under the band policy. Many of the husbands of these women are not Indians, but they will be living in the villages.

Now, with the changes in the Indian Act, the Indian women get to remain "Indian" even if they marry non-Indian husbands. Because of these changes, there are going to be white men living on the reserves as well as white women. With the new law, it is up to each band to decide if they want their own membership rules. All bands can now decide who will be allowed to be members. Our band rules say that you have to have Indian blood in you before you can apply to be a member.

The way I see it it has worked pretty good in the past for our men who married non-native women and brought them here to the village to live. The government wants everything equal for men and women but to me it will not be equal and the same. The men who marry non-Indian women stay in the village where they were born. Our men worked for

Plate 36
Don Assu signs a Treaty of Peace and Alliance on behalf of the Nuyumbalees Society with a representative of the Ainu Cultural Society from Hokkaido, Japan, at the Kwagiulth Museum during the Kwagiulth and Ainu cultural exchange in 1985. Photo by Estelle Inman

this village. Times are changing, and women are running for positions on the band councils now, but it is the men who have handled our affairs. Almost every man here is fishing, no matter what other job he has, so when he speaks at our meeting, he knows what he is talking about. It is only in the past few years that non-native women began to live here with their husbands and raise families. To me that's okay.

In our villages the men stay, and women come in from other places. That works out fine. The women stay pretty close to home with their kids, and only a few have other jobs. They have Indian status and are members of the band. Here in the village, they work with all the women for the good of the village, especially the children. They have fitted in with our way of doing things.

What I wonder is how it will work out now that Indian women can stay here when they marry a non-native man, and these men come to live in the community. There are already large numbers of families planning to come back. The government made that change in the law retroactive so that women who left the village to marry out, no matter how long ago, can return if they want to. At Cape Mudge our numbers could double. At Campbell River, more families than now live on reserve could come in there. It could be that on some small reserves in B.C. non-native men could outnumber Indian men. So what bothers me is keeping control over our own community and our affairs.

If the band councils don't choose to make up their own rules for membership in the band, non-Indians could apply for membership in the band, and if a majority voted them in, they would attend meetings, share in band funds, and even run for office on the band council. Then what would happen to our control over our own affairs?

I've been in a lot of meetings of our people over my lifetime where a few white men are attending. Women mostly don't speak, no matter who they are. They vote, but they don't tell other people how to vote. Non-native men want to talk all the time, so even if they don't know anything about our history or fishing or our way of doing things, they would want to speak in meetings. They talk like lawyers! They never seem to know who by rights should be speaking.

So in many native bands they will be voting on their own band membership rules. We've done that here at Cape Mudge. You must be Indian to apply to be a member of the band. A couple of other bands in the Kwagiulth District have done that too. Others had better be watching that they don't lose control over their own affairs. The independence of our people that we have been fighting for all our lives could be lost from inside the community over time.

7
Renewal of the Potlatch at Cape Mudge

Many of the Kwagiulth people were arrested for taking part in a big pot-latch given by Dan Cranmer on Village Island in 1921. Dan's wife Emma was from Village Island, and her family were giving away a lot of things that went into that potlatch because that's what the family is expected to do for the daughter who is married. My father and eldest brother Dan were called to go there because my father was related to Emma. I don't know if anyone else went from the villages around here.

My father and brother were arrested. Charges were laid against them under a law that had been on the books for a long time. They were told they would go to jail unless they signed a paper that said they wouldn't potlatch any more. They were told that our people would have to hand over everything they used for the potlatch, whether they were there or not. Anybody arrested who didn't give up their family's masks and other things went to jail. Twenty-two of our Kwagiulth people went to Oakalla. They were prisoners from two months to six months.[1]

My father had to go to court in Alert Bay two or three times. I was only a young fellow then, and I wasn't too concerned – older men were handling it anyway; but I remember thinking, "Why would the Indian agent start all that?" I was around seventeen at the time and walked every day to Quathiaski Cove from the village and back home at night after spending all day learning to use machine tools with W. E. Anderson. He was the manager and the best mechanic we had at the cannery. I felt lucky to learn and was working hard at it. I didn't know what the government was doing to our people, taking away our culture.

The scow came around from the cannery and put in at the village to pick up the big pile of masks and headdresses and belts and coppers – everything we had for potlatching. I saw it pull out across Discovery Passage to the Campbell River side where more stuff was loaded on the *Princess Beatrice* for the trip to Alert Bay. Alert Bay was where the potlatch gear was gathered together. It came mainly from our village around here and from Alert Bay and Village Island. It was sent to the museum in Ottawa from Alert Bay by the Indian agent. Our old people who watched the barge pull out from shore with all their masks on it said: "There is nothing left now. We might as well go home." When we say "go home," it means to die.

When that shipment went to Ottawa they were supposed to send $1,415 to pay for all the things our Kwagiulth people had been forced to give up under threat of jail. But people are still alive who didn't get paid and they never knew anybody who did get paid. You can't buy *one* of those old pieces now for $1,415! They took away around six hundred pieces.

A collector named Heye turned up at Alert Bay, and the Indian agent Halliday sold him some of our stuff before he shipped off the rest to the museum in Ottawa.[2] Even the government who were getting all the rest didn't like that! They wanted it all for themselves, I guess. Heye had his pick of all those hundreds and hundreds of pieces. One of them belonged to my father; some to my grandfather, Jim Naknakim; to my wife's uncle, John Dick; and to other Lekwiltok men in this area, as well as people from farther north at Alert Bay and Village Island. None of the pieces that went to Heye's museum in New York were ever returned though we sent a delegation there to negotiate with them.

In 1978 the National Museum in Ottawa returned the part of the collection they still held because they knew it was wrong to force us to stop our custom of potlatching and take all our goods away from us. But early on Indian Affairs had gone ahead and loaned around 135 pieces of our masks and regalia to the Royal Ontario Museum, and it took us much longer to get that museum to return what is ours. This is our family inheritance I am talking about. You don't give up on that! Finally, in 198 the Royal Ontario Museum returned what they had taken.

Our people figured that all that potlatch gear that was taken away to museums was still theirs by rights and that they still owned it, so it would have to be given back. Those old people kept trying to have it returned to them. A lot of people worked to get it back. I know Jimmy Sewid went to Ottawa with Guy Williams in 1963, and he went into the museum for the Kwagiulth people and demanded our stuff back. He had his wife's mother with him to be sure of what was ours. He told them h

late 37
ne of a series of photographs
produced from glass plates showing
e "potlatch" collection on display in
e church hall in Alert Bay in 1922.
any of these items have now been
turned from Ottawa and Toronto and
e on display in the museums at Cape
udge and Alert Bay. Photo by V. S.
ord (PN 12191 RBCM)

was ready to buy it back for the $1,415 they claimed to have paid for
and to bring a truck around and load it in; and he told them he was read
to go to the newspapers and tell how the museum had got hold of ou
stuff.

Back then, they wouldn't show us the potlatch regalia or liste
Finally, in 1973 they informed our chiefs' meeting in the Kwakiutl Di
trict Council that they were going to return the "Potlatch Collection
But they didn't want to give it back to the families who own it. The
wanted it put in a museum. So it was voted that the museum should b
built at Cape Mudge. Well, the Nimpkish band at Alert Bay wanted th
museum to be built up there. So in the end two museums were buil
and each museum could show what was taken away from their ow
area. Village Islanders had to decide where their goods would go becaus
they didn't live on Village Island anymore.

Here at Cape Mudge we set up the Nuyumbalees Society to get a mu
seum going and bring back the potlatch regalia. We chose the nam
Kwagiulth Museum because we wanted it to be for all our people no
just our Lekwiltok tribe. At Cape Mudge we are located where a
people can easily call in on their way down from our northern villages t
the city – Victoria or Vancouver. It's a good place for getting togethe
Nuyumbalees means "the beginning of all legends." The legends are th
history of our families. That is why the chiefs show our dances in th
potlatch, so that our legends are passed on to the people.

It has all worked out pretty well. All our stuff that was brought bac
from Ottawa is in glass cases in the museum according to the family th
owns them. That's what the masks and other things mean to us: fami
ownership. We are proud of that! It tells our family rights to the peopl
With our people you don't talk about what rights to dances you've go
you call the people and show them in the potlatch. A few families ha
only a few pieces of what was taken away from their family returned ar
put in the museum. That wasn't right, and they were really angry. That
another reason why *all* the pieces that were taken away in 1922 and a
in museums in Canada and other countries have to be brought back.

On museum opening day, 29 June 1979, my son Don brought h
seiner around to the beach in front of the museum. Chiefs of all ou
Kwagiulth villages were on board, drumming and singing. Jim Sew
was our speaker. He welcomed everybody from the beach. There we
about five hundred people. He called to the chiefs of each band in ou
language, welcoming the people from that village.

That's when they threw "Klassila," the spirit of dancing, from th
boat to the shore, where it was caught by a fellow who started up dan

Figure 12
*Two Gakula masks from the Billy Assu
Collection (Left, 979.1.112 and right,
971.1.71 KM). Drawings by Hilary
Stewart, 1985*

ing. Then he threw it back up and into the museum.[3]

Everyone moved up the beach and around the ramp outside the museum doors. We didn't have a ribbon cutting. That's not our custom. We had a cedar-bark cutting. The chiefs were holding a long piece of dyed red cedar bark in a circle. I chose Colleen Dick from Cape Mudge to be our princess and stand in the middle of the ring. She is the daughter of two families with a lot of masks on display in the museum. Her father was Dick, and her mother is Assu.

All the important people pressed close in to the bark ring so that nobody saw the knife passed hand to hand. The cedar bark was slashed and there was a scream. All the chiefs got excited, and each shouted out the cries of the animals they can show in the potlatch: the Whales blew, the Bears growled, the Hamatsas cried out. It sounded like a big roar.

When the museum doors were opened, the chiefs came first, followed by the people. Everybody was given a piece of the cedar ring as they came inside, just the way it was done in the old days. Then our chiefs gathered in the open space in the middle of the museum. After fifty-seven years we had our family possessions back! A big shout went up. It was the sound of Klassila, the spirit of dancing, now back again in the house.

My boys and I put up a totem pole to my father inside the museum. Sam Henderson and his sons carved it with Assu family crests. It's big and heavy, around twenty-nine feet tall and fifteen hundred pounds. It had to be lowered in from above before the museum roof was put on. When you raise a pole you have to potlatch. I potlatched for all the tribes when they gathered here for the museum opening. Our fishermen donated the salmon we roasted over the open fires for everybody – fifteen hundred pounds.

A year later another pole was put out in the open area outside the museum and beside the entrance door. That pole was carved by Sam Henderson and his sons and has the crests of their family on it. Sam was from Blunden Harbour, but he married the oldest daughter of Johnny Quocksister of Campbell River, and they raised their family over there. When he put up that pole, there was another big celebration when the Hendersons called the people to the potlatch.

The museum has been good for the Kwagiulth people. Our people who want to learn about native customs come to the museum. When the Ainu or Hawaiians or other people come to visit, we bring them here. Many of our young people have been trained to teach school classes and the public in the museum. They are learning the Kwakwala language, and there is carving, dancing, button-blanket-making, and work with cedar bark. They learn about the potlatch and how everything was used. The elders teach it to the kids. One of the museum programs won first prize for a program in the schools.

I've been on the museum board from the start. I think that getting our potlatch goods back has done a lot to teach our youth who we really are. It will help us to hold on to our history.

My wife Ida and I raised seven children and have twenty-four grandchildren and thirty-one great-grandchildren. At my birthday on 14 Feb-

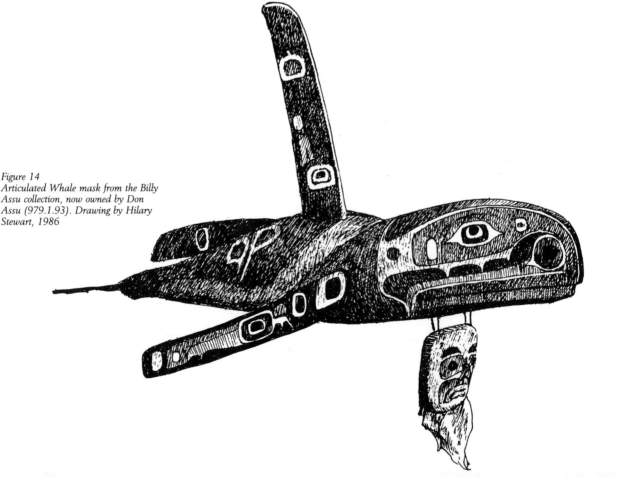

Figure 14
Articulated Whale mask from the Billy
Assu collection, now owned by Don
Assu (979.1.93). Drawing by Hilary
Stewart, 1986

ruary 1986, our family gave a dinner party and sixty-one relatives attended.

Back in May 1977, we held a feast and called all our family members to it. We gave out names to sons and daughters, grandsons and granddaughters, nieces and nephews, and great-grandchildren. These names had been passed down in our family for generations. Names came from our great-grandparents, our grandparents, and their sisters and brothers; some came from our nieces' and nephews' grandparents – from both sides of the family.

About a year after I was born, my people gave a small potlatch for me in my grandfather's house. When I was ten years old, more was given to me in a family potlatch, and I received my boy-name. This name is x̌aṅaǧəmaẏa, meaning "top giver." After my father's death, his name yax̌nəkʷaʔas came to me. I now hold the name ʔewanukʷ, which came to me with the gift of a copper from Jim Sewid at my last potlatch.

To give our names we invited everybody in our family to a dinner in the community hall at Cape Mudge. Ida and I wore our Klassila head-dresses and button blankets. Jim Sewid's daughter Daisy acted as our speaker in giving away the names. Those related to us like the Cliftons and the Sewids also gave some names to grandchildren related to them. After dinner, when all the family were still at the tables, the names were called out. Each person got a card with his name written on it. Special names are given to people who are in line for them in the family. I gave out quite a bit of money. That's our potlatch custom to do that.

When you continue the names of the people in the family who have gone before, you feel part of something bigger that goes way back in time. Some of our people believed in reincarnation. I know I still do. Maybe that is part of why this custom is so important to us. But mainly it is important because it keeps the family together, the way we want it to be. We want them to be strong in the Indian culture.

My biggest potlatch was a memorial potlatch to honour my wife Ida. After she died, our families spent a year getting ready to call all the people. The potlatch has different parts. It starts with the sad songs for those who have died, then if coppers are given, there is a really nice happy time. That is followed by the serious Red Cedar Bark Ceremonies.[4] People from different villages come to show the dances they have a right to. Next comes the Klassila where the chiefs from different tribes dance for the people, and there is a lot of fun. It is peaceful then. That's the part I always liked best. At the end we hand out all the money and goods that have been gathered together for the people who take part.

Our potlatches start with q̓asa. It means crying. My wife was loved and respected by all our family and everyone who knew her. Everyone feels sad to see the elders die because they are the ones who are carrying on our custom of the potlatch today. Ida's close friends and relatives were the mourners. These women wearing button blankets sat down in a line at the back of the hall facing the people.

During the year after Ida's death I didn't say her name. That's an old custom of our people, and I don't know how many others keep it still. Speaking the name brings that person too close for comfort – like calling them back. We had other customs here at time of death such as burning the things that belonged to the dead. They did that when I was a boy. Before my time, women used to meet in a secret place in the woods to cry and scratch their faces and tear out their hair. If a song-maker over heard this crying, he could make up a song out of the sounds, and that song would be sung when all the people gathered at the potlatch in her honour. When I was a boy, the women here still cut ten inches off their hair when one of their "sisters" died.

Some of these mourning songs are remembered in each tribe and sung every year at potlatches. Bill Hunt of Fort Rupert led off at my potlatch with the first song. All the singers were with him, and they followed him and beat time. That song was made to honour a great chief of that tribe nəqaʔbənkəm. It is a name that later went to Mungo Martin. You can hear the word ʔum̓alał repeated over and over in the song. It means "noble lady" because they were singing it for Ida. If a man had died, the word "gigəme" would have been used. Jim King thanked the Fort Ruperts for me. Adam Dick of Kingcome Inlet was my speaker for the night, but he came late, so at first Jimmy King thanked the singers and dancers and those who stood up to speak for Ida. Every village used to have a speaker for potlatches. At Cape Mudge it was Tom Wallace for our people.

One of the next mourning songs told about six noblemen who left Quatsino Sound on a sailing ship and never came back. J. J. Wallace of Quatsino led that song.

The third set of songs came from the West Coast people. Roy Hamilton led the singers. Everybody likes West Coast songs. They have a really good tune in them.

Next, the Campbell River people paid their respects to Ida with a song Sam Henderson had made up when his wife (May Quocksister) died. May and Sam are dead now, but the song had been taped so that Henry George of c̓əlgʷadi was able to sing along with it and lead the other singers.

ure 15
ief Harry Assu's copper quluma.
erpretive illustration by Hilary
wart, 1986

Jim Sewid led off with the last of the mourning songs sung in honour of Ida. Jim's father was qʷiqʷəsutinux̌ʷ from Gilford Island, and his mother was məməliliqəla from Village Island. The song he sang came down from the Rivers Inlet people to the people of Village Island. It is called "Lament of the Nobles."[5] It is about the spirit of the loved one travelling all around the world. While this song was being sung, all the mourners stood up and swayed slowly. We call that ƛeq̓ʷala, meaning we will shake off our sorrows. Well, that's the time for everybody to change over. We have to cheer up now because all relatives and friends have come down here to be with our family in time of trouble.

After the mourning ceremony came the giving of coppers to me. I didn't know anything about it beforehand so I was really surprised! A "copper" is a big shield made of copper metal with a design on it. Every copper has a name. They are bought for a higher and higher price each time they are sold. It has gone on for so long that some are worth thousands of dollars. Jim Sewid gave me a copper.[6]

The name of my copper is quluma. It is so old that the meaning has been lost. Jim Sewid got it from his uncle Henry Bell, who passed it on to Jim before he died a few years ago. Before that it belonged to Jim's grandfather, Jim Bell from Village Island.

Jim and Flora Sewid's daughter Louisa is married to our son Don, and she is a member of the Cape Mudge band. That is why her father gave me a copper. It honours Louisa among our people. It is not right for a father to give nothing to his daughter's husband and family. It would be a

disgrace for her. Jim Sewid was giving to me and my family as a dowr
for Louisa. That's the way we all back up the marriage.

Jim and Flora Sewid and Ida and I have four grandsons by Don an
Louisa: Brian, Patrick, Michael, and Bradley. What is given to me by th
Sewids will go to my son Don when I die and then on to our (mutua)
grandchildren. So when you receive wealth in a potlatch, it is like mak
ing a will. You have to do that in front of all the people so that thes
rights are known.

Louisa and Don stood at the centre of our two families when the cop
per was given in her name. She was dressed with cedar bark headdres
with ermine tails and button blanket. J. J. Wallace was speaker for Jim
so he announced the copper was given to me. A great name was given t
me with the copper. The name is ʔewanuk*. It means (a chief is
"watching the point" (for the arrival of his guests at the potlatch).

Then my son Don was given one of the greatest names the Sewic
own. That name is ƛəliliƛa. It is a Gilford Island name meanin
"always inviting." My son will use that name, and it will be passed on t
his sons.

Next Jim Sewid had it announced that he would supid a copper t
me. Supid means "pass on." The copper is given to me and is the
bought back by Jim so that it stays in his family. Every time the copper
bought its price goes up; so Jim gave me even more than the copper ha
been worth before, and that money went toward putting on this po
latch. The name of the copper supid to me is lubiƛila. That means "ever
cent went to buying it." Jim Sewid's uncle Henry Bell had owned it b
fore. He had bought it from yəqiʌəsm̓e, the father-in-law of Har
Mountain.

The old ladies who know all about how these things are done wer
dancing. Now that coppers were given to honour my daughter-in-lav
Louisa can wear copper shapes outlined in buttons on her blanket.

More coppers were supid to me. Willie Cranmer of Alert Bay came u
and handed me a copper named ʔənq*əla, meaning "Foggy." It used t
belong to Wakius at Alert Bay. The copper was taken away with the re
of the stuff for potlatching in 1922, but it has been returned. When th
copper was supid to me, it was bought back right then, and the mon
went into the bag with the rest to give out at this potlatch.

Paul Willie of Kingcome Inlet brought up another copper to supid t
me. The name of this copper is ʔisəməla. That means "Abalone Face."
was bought back then and more money to be given away was paid ov
for it.

Adam Dick from Kingcome Inlet brought a copper to supid to m but he arrived too late to hand it over, so his mother gave it to me and bought it back again, so all that went into putting on my potlatch.

All these chiefs who suṗid coppers are important to my family. At the end Louisa presented me with the copper quluma, which Jim Sewid gave me outright, while a special song was sung. It says how her "brothers" came from far away to give coppers to her father-in-law. Then the women danced. Only those who had been married in the Indian way danced out in front of the people.

In the old days the chiefs brought coppers to the potlatches in case they had to sue somebody who tried to take away their place and grab it for himself. Then the chief would break a copper, and if that man couldn't do the same, he would have to back down. It's a lot different now. Nowadays they bring their coppers to the potlatch to honour people.

The next part of the potlatch is the Red Cedar Bark Ceremony. It's the dark side of our history that is being danced. All the dancers come out from behind a painted cloth screen. Guests don't go there because you are not supposed to know who is dancing the masks (of supernatural beings). In our big family there were so many dancers we needed two screens. Dora Cook painted one screen especially for this potlatch. Dora was back there telling the people when to get dressed and when to come out. There were so many people, she said it only worked because four generations were working together. So many dances were shown that a list was made and pinned up on the back of a screen. That was the first time that was ever done. It will be hard to remember all the dances that were shown at my potlatch.[7]

The most important dance in the Red Cedar Bark Ceremony is Hamatsa. My eldest son Steve danced that – top dancer. It was the Hamatsa ritual that Jim Sewid gave me and the second time Steve danced it. Jim gave him the name ʔənqalis to go with the Hamatsa Dance. That's the name Jim was given when he first was made a hamatsa dancer when he was a boy. It means "opening the mouth for food."

When the Hamatsa begins, you hear the whistles blowing. That's the sound of the cannibal monster bəxbəxwəlanusiwe.[8] Then the hamatsa dancer appears from behind the screen. The power of the monster is on him, and he is hungry for human flesh because that's the food of the cannibal he met on his spirit quest. He is wild and out of control and has to be caught and brought back to his senses.

Adam Dick came out carrying two red cedar bark neck-rings to use to capture the hamatsa when they found him. Jim Sewid walked slowly be-

hind him, shaking the round rattle that gives power to the neck-ring
When they got to Steve, they threw the neck-rings over his head an
Steve shouted "hap!" "hap!" (food, food) and plunged off into the fou
corners of the dance floor. He circled around four times before the sing
ing and drumming and whistling ended. Then he went off behind th
screens. For those Red Cedar Bark dances everyone whirls around on th
spot as they go in or come out from the screens. It's our custom; yo
have to do that.

Then the whistles blew again, and the songs and drumming starte
up, and Steve came out for the second time as hamatsa. My speaker wa
calling out to him not to fall, or he would disgrace our family and a cop
per would have to be broken. His sister Audrey danced backward befor
him holding out her arms as if she was offering him food. She is h
conscience – she is trying to cool him off. Audrey was his heliga?, h
leader. Then other women joined Audrey in trying to bring the hamats
back to his senses, and men went with him too because once in a whil
he would break away and cry out, crouch down, and struggle to ge
away.

Next time the hamatsa came again, he carried my copper quluma
The whistles were sounding, and in the loud singing and drumming an
shouting, he started getting wild again. He put the copper in the middl
of the floor, and all the high-ranking people who have been mad
hamatsas came out to dance with him around it and support him.

After that they showed the dance of the həmsəmɬ, the bird monster
who feed the cannibal bəxbəxʷəlanusiwe. First is hux̌ʷhuqʷ. You're no
supposed to know who dances the masks, but you can guess because th
Hendersons of Campbell River carved those masks. Bobby Joseph cam
out with the dancer to help him because it is hard to see behind th
mask, and the mask is so heavy that the dancer might fall. Next cam
ǧaluqʷəmɬ, crooked beak. Dick Joseph of Turnour Island was with th
dancer to help. Next dancer was Raven. They all danced at the sam
time with their wooden beaks lifting and banging down. At the last an
other crooked beak came out – so there were four cannibal birds. This i
the most exciting part of the Hamatsa ritual with singing, fast, har
drumming, whistles, and the birds all out on the floor together.[9]

After that was finished, Mrs. M. Cook of Alert Bay had it announce
by Willie Cranmer that she would be giving the potlatch next year.

My eldest grandson, Rod Naknakim, came out next dancing the stor
of a man who came out of the sea. That spirit was afraid of fire so he wa
always trying to put out the fire. Rod wore a neck-ring of twisted yellov
and red cedar bark. He was being attracted by fire, and his attendant

Plate 38
Audrey Wilson, sister of the Hamatsa Stephen Assu, dances backward before him in an attempt to calm him. Photo taken at Harry Assu's potlatch on 9 June 1984. Courtesy Campbell River Courier

had to hold on to him so that he didn't burn himself. He kept rushing at the "fire" to stamp on it, to put it out. The dance is really old and always shown with the hamatsa if the person giving the potlatch has the right to it.

Even a little child can be made hamatsa. Nicole Assu is Don and Louisa's granddaughter by their eldest son Brian and his wife Tami. She was brought out by Vera Cranmer and Ethel Alfred, and she danced around the floor. Agnes Alfred gave her the name yaqusəlagəlis. That was the name the old lady was given when she was made hamatsa as a young girl. She's over a hundred years old now. It is a Village Island name and was passed down to Dora Cook, then Dora gave up the name and her place in the Hamatsa to Nicole.

In the next dance, rich woman was shown. She is ǧuminəwaǧas, a spirit from the forest wearing hemlock branches on her head. Other women came out with her, and Bobby Joseph and Ron Hamilton came with her. My niece Violet Duncan from Campbell River was ǧuminəwaǧas. Violet is a high-ranking lady, the daughter of my sister Susan, who was married to Johnny Quocksister of Campbell River. The singers and drummers keep everything going, and every time a dance is over, the speaker announces how the right to show it came into the fam-

ily, who owns the dance. The way these dances spread out to the Kwagiulth people was by marriage dowries.

The ghost dancer was next. My daughter Pearl danced that for the people. Older women were out on the floor to guide her.

Then five of my grandchildren did the Wolf Dance. Some wore wolf headdresses. They lined up in a row and danced up and down in their places. You can tell it is the Wolf Dance by the songs and because the dancers keep their thumbs up.

The Ghost Dance was followed by a dance that came into our family long ago by marriage to a family from the West Coast. It is called ʔaʔumalał. The high-ranking lady dancer, Deane Le Fleur, wore a big cedar hat. She can throw sickness into people and cure them again. Of course, after each dance, the speaker has to tell where the dance came from and the name that is given to the dancer with it. If he forgets, one of the old ladies will go over to him and get after him.

In the next performance, all the dancers wore white. It is called ṅəṅalał, the Day Dance. The fringes on their costumes moved as they danced slowly in a line. They greet the day. This was danced by the wives of my grandsons. The speaker told where this dance came from and announced the names given to the dancers.

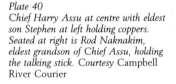

Plate 40
Chief Harry Assu at centre with eldest son Stephen at left holding coppers. Seated at right is Rod Naknakim, eldest grandson of Chief Assu, holding the talking stick. Courtesy Campbell River Courier

One of my young granddaughters, Wendy Dick, danced the tuʔxʷid. She turned her button blanket inside out because a plain blanket used to be used for this dance. She wore hemlock branches on her head. Katy Ferrie of Campbell River guided her because she is so young and hadn't danced it before. The song sung for this dance is "I Have Been All over the Earth." The people tease the dancer because she claims she has gone all around the world and returned with a ƛugʷe (treasure) of magic. They try to get her to show it to them. Then she danced slowly backward toward the screens, and you could see a big wooden frog following her across the floor. That was a surprise, and everybody was laughing. She proved her magic power all right!

There were so many dances that I have lost track of them. My speaker, Adam Dick, asked the drummers to hang on to their sticks because at this rate they might all have to stay all night. I remember there was the Professional Dance, where the singers and drummers keep changing the beat so the line of women dancers have to know how to follow. That dance was led by Lucy Onley. All sides of our families joined in.

Another dance was the x̌ʷix̌ʷi. Two men came out shaking shell rattles and scattering coins to the kids. Their masks were carved by Bill Holm. That dance came to our people from the Comox.

After that there was the Paddle Dance. This is a women's dance, and all my relatives joined into it. After paddling all around the floor, they ended up by bailing at the stern with a plastic bucket. It's a lot of fun to see.

The ʔuniqʷa dancer is the one who doesn't want anyone else coming out and dancing with her. She stops dancing if they do. She can look into the future and heal the people. My granddaughter Colleen Dick danced that. Colleen has been given my mother's name, m̓axʷaʔugʷa.

Twenty-four grandchildren came out next dancing to the tune of a song composed by nəqaʔbənkəm of Fort Rupert. The speaker thanked them for dancing and told where that song had come from.

The Mountain Goat hunter came on next. It was danced by my grandson Rick. He went round the floor carrying a long pole with a noose on it. As the drums beat faster and faster, the head of a mountain goat shot up above the screens, and the hunter made a run at it. It's a very important dance, that dance, and Jim Sewid received it as dowry when he married his wife Flora. It came long ago from Jack Peters of New Vancouver village.

One of the last dances in the Cedar Bark Series was the Salmon Dance. Any family that has twins can do the Salmon Dance. Our people said that twins are salmon. My granddaughter Colleen Dick has twins, so

Plate 41
Patrick Assu dances the Mountain Goat hunter. Assu family album, 1984

she led out the dancers. The Sewids have twins, Emma and Mabel, so
they were the body of the Salmon in the middle of the line. Their sister
Lucy Onley led that Salmon Dance. After the Sewid twins were born,
there were no other twins born, so this Salmon Dance does not have a
tail. The Hendersons in Campbell River have two sets of twins, so they
can dance the whole Salmon. Others joined into the line of dancers to
show respect for the families giving the dance. J. J. Wallace led the song
for the Salmon Dance.

Another very important dance was məʔdəm. It tells the story of a boy
who went out alone along Woss Lake, where he was given a ƛugʷe (treasure). He saw crystals rolling down the mountain there. From them he
got his power to fly. At one time, the man who could do this dance was
pulled up to the beams of the big house with leather strips through cuts
on his back and knees. That is why my grandson Patrick, kept looking up
ing up into the beams above while he was dancing. Long ago I saw them
pulling up a dancer here at Cape Mudge. It was Paddy Grey's father. His
grandfather too had the right to that.

The war dancer came on about that time. He was carrying a big sea-
serpent board in his arms. It was danced by my grandson Michael, and
he was the warrior spirit, sisiyuƛ. Michael wore the headdress of a
chief; ermine skins on a cedar bark band. This is an important dance.

A Grizzly Bear spirit came out next. This dance is high up too. It was
danced by Bradley Assu, fourth son of Don and Louisa. He received a
name from Jim Sewid, who owns this dance and has given me the right
to have it shown by my family.

For the last great event in the Red Cedar Bark Ceremony, my son Mel
came out in a black blanket, carrying my copper quluma. He is helagalis,
and he is making Raven's cry. This tells the chiefs that Raven will peck

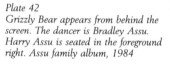

Plate 42
Grizzly Bear appears from behind the screen. The dancer is Bradley Assu. Harry Assu is seated in the foreground right. Assu family album, 1984

the copper into pieces if my rights to the coppers, songs, dances, and names that have come down in the family are challenged. The challenger would have to break a copper too or lose out.

Well, the Red Cedar Bark Ceremony was over, and there was a big roar of drumming and shouting. The song leader was calling "Wa!" and the singers were shouting out "Yi!" Everyone was shouting it out! It means "let's roll over" from the dark side of the ċeʔqa to the ƛaʔsala.

The Kwagiulth people really love Klassila. That's when we do the "Peace Dance" or "Feather Dance." It came down to us from the northern people – Bella Bella and Bella Coola. Chiefs who have come to the potlatch to honour the host come out in long lines and dance with their families for the people. They wear the ermine headdresses and blankets and aprons. Each time a different family comes out to dance, and then they show some ƛugʷe (treasure) that they have a right to show the people.

Everybody used to be very quiet and respectful in the old days, and there was no talking or walking around the house at Klassilas. Nowadays everybody is enjoying themselves, and some of the dances are really funny, so that I don't think it is so serious any more, after the opening part.

Brian Assu, my grandson, who is the oldest of the four sons of Don and Louisa was holikəłał. He comes out first. He is the boss – leader of the Klassila and equal to the Hamatsa in the Red Cedar Bark Ceremony. Brian is kʷikʷ, Eagle of the tribe. Adam Dick came out with Brian. He was shaking the round rattles. That makes it sacred. Brian has been given the right to use that rattle. This privilege that Brian is showing came down from Rivers Inlet. Agnes Alfred came out to help Brian because he got this right through her. Jim Sewid led the song that was his grandfather Sewid's song.

When the rattles sounded, a line of chiefs from my family came out – all grandsons. Tony Roberts, my daughter Jean's son, led them in to dance the Feather Dance. J. J. Wallace led a song that says, "He is going around the house looking for a ƛugʷe." Mungo Martin made that song. After they danced the Feather Dance, one of the Webber boys from the Tsulquade tribe started pestering a chief in the line of dancers. The one they choose is someone close to the family giving the potlatch. This time it was Bobby Assu, and he went out of the hall. You could hear noises outside the building. Webber came back carrying the chief's blanket and headdress – the chief had disappeared! Then in came ǧʷəyəm, a Whale. Drumming was kept up all the time the Whale was danced around the house. Adam Dick's father carved that Whale mask.

After that, the next line of chiefs came out to honour our family, and after they danced, they got teased by the two boys from Tsulquade, and Bobby Joseph left the hall. Somebody brought in his headdress and blanket and said he had gone. Then back came the ʌugʷe, out from behind the screens. It was Echo. Under his blanket the Echo had mouthpieces of Komoqua (rich ruler of the wealth of the sea), Grizzly Bear, Sea-Egg (Urchin), Starfish, Raven, and Thunderbird. Every time he turned away and turned back again, he showed a different animal face. This mask had been carved by Jimmy Dick too. Jim Sewid and J. J. Wallace led the songs.

So, that is the way Klassila is done. The Henderson family came in next to dance Klassila, and after Bill Henderson was taken away, his ʌugʷe was shown: dᶻunuq̓ʷa (wild woman of the woods).

In the dance that followed the full moon and the half moon fought over which should be in the sky. They danced for the people, and the winner was decided by which got the loudest applause. It was really funny. They even danced the Twist! Lelooska, an artist from the States, made those masks.

Agnes Cranmer and Margaret Cook and a group of women came and danced the Peace Dance for the people. Lisa Wells was taken away, and two dancers came back wearing a "mother" and a "father" mask. They carried a cradle. It had a wooden baby in it. The baby sat up in the cradle when strings were pulled.

After the next line of chiefs came in for the Peace Dance, everything was interrupted by some "visitors." These uninvited Gakula are clowns who haven't been invited. They can't seem to keep their pants up. After they warmed their backsides at the "fire," they were made to dance and then they were kicked out. You can't Klassila with those clowns around.

Another line of nobles came out led by Bobby Joseph, and the ʌugʷe for this dance was a different dᶻunuq̓ʷa, wild woman of the woods.

Well, for the ending, I led out the line of my family to Klassila with me: Rod Naknakim, Mel, Don and Louisa, Shirley Vrable, and my eldest daughter Audrey, who held the talking stick. A song from the West Coast people was sung and led by Ron Hamilton, who later spoke highly of my father and our family. Then women were standing up speaking for Ida and her family. Jim Sewid spoke again for us, and others spoke of the important history of our family.

Then all our family and supporters danced around the floor. They were really happy. They were waving towels and pillows and money to be given away. That's when the big gift-giving starts. That's what th potlatch is famous for.

We give to those people who came to sing and dance and speak for us and to all those who came to the potlatch. Things to give away were stacked up in the middle of the hall, and our family carried them to the people. Usually the old people and those who have done most of the planning for the potlatch go with those who are handing out the money and goods to be sure that people who have helped the family most are taken care of: the singers and those who showed their dances and helped out with the whole thing. Some of those who helped most were women in our family, so I bought pearl necklaces for them when I was in Hong Kong. They were given bouquets of carnations.

Well it was around nine-thirty or ten o'clock when the potlatch was over. There was still light in the west. You know, some of our people used to wonder whether the potlatch was a good thing or not. When I think about that potlatch now, I know it was good.

Notes

Notes to Chapter One

1 The writing system for the Indian words in this book is explained in Appendix 1.
2 When it is mentioned in notes and publications by social scientists, this village is usually spelled Tekya. It is a designated archaeological site (EdSk-6). Descendants of the Northern Strait of Georgia Salish who occupied the site in earliest times say that Tekya is a Comox word meaning "close one eye and squirt" (personal communication, Bouchard and Kennedy, 1986).
3 Since the name of weqaʔi is spelled Wai-Kai by the We-Wai-Kai band, this spelling will be used.
4 Other dates for the establishment of a We-Wai-Kai village at Cape Mudge are after 1860 (Curtis 1915: 105) and circa 1845 (Duff and Taylor 1956: 63).
5 *North Island Gazette*, 14 November 1984.
6 According to Harry Assu's father, Billy Assu, the Nimpkish village referred to was hwulk, visited by Captain Vancouver in 1792 and renamed Cheslaklee by him for a head man he met there (Drucker, field notes, 1953, N.A.A.). In a later interview with Drucker, Billy Assu gave the source of the many coppers in a box that were brought to hwulk at the mouth of the Nimpkish River as dowry. The edited account is as follows: "Wīqe married a woman from Gilford Island q̓ehwuqʔanux. She told him [that her] father had Lōkwola, a copper.

   Wulásu was old man's name, he had boil on back. He dreamed that [if he would] stand watch at low-time – [he] would find a medicine. At night [he] saw light from the beach [and] went and lay in [it] and healed his back. Under was melted copper – he put [it] in basket. [The melted copper was] made [in a] form to shape into [a ceremonial] copper. He made [a] bundle of five coppers to sent to Wīqe; Wīqe called some people and gave away the first one.

   The old man tried to make [a] big box so big couldn't lift – put in canoe and [it was] filled with coppers. . . . No one, not even two [men] could lift box at hwulk." (Drucker, field notes, 1955).
7 The spelling "lekwiltok" is used as an alternate rendering of lig̱ʷiłdaʔx̌ʷ, as spoken by Harry Assu. Edward Curtis (1910) translated the word to mean "unkillable thing" and noted that it was also applied to "a large sea worm, which cannot be killed by cutting in pieces, for the separate parts go wriggling off through the water." Franz Boas interpreted the meaning of this tribal name as "Fire of the House" from which he derived from the root: "ləgwiʔł" ("Kwakiutl Grammar," new series, 1947: 328).
8 While it has been recorded that the Comox moved south from their territory north of Kye Bay on Vancouver Island into what is now Courtenay Bay at Comox to take

over the territory left vacant by the Salish Pentlatch tribe (who had previousl
owned the area but who had been decimated by the West Coast tribes) and tha
subsequently the Lekwiltok spread farther to the south (Boas 1887: 131), there i
also considerable evidence that the Comox were forced out of their northern terri
tory by the southern movement of the Lekwiltok (Duff and Taylor 1956: 60). N
doubt both pull and push were factors in the Comox removal to Courtenay Bay

9 The native reserve at Comox, long the home of Vancouver Island-Comox speaker
predominantly, has been described in the literature as the northernmost village c
the Comox. With amalgamation with the Salmon River Lekwiltok and the dyin
out of the Comox language, the village today is socially and politically Kwagiulth

10 A local name frequently used for Tsquloten is "playing field." It has been trans
lated as "Indian-game place" by Kennedy and Bouchard in *Sliammon Life, Sliam
mon Lands* (169) and as "shinny stick" by Wayne Suttles (personal communica
tion, 1985).

11 According to an account by Franz Boas published in The 35th Annual Report o
the Bureau of American Ethnology, Smithsonian Institution, 1913–1914, a mar
riage took place between a Pentlatch boy named Nem Nemen (whose parent
could not find a suitable mate for him amongst the Comox at Courtenay Bay) and
princess of a chief of the We-Wai-Kai at Tsquloten, presumably the present villag
of Cape Mudge, where they came to reside. The number of generations that fol
lowed on that marriage up until the opening of the Hudson's Bay fort at For
Rupert in 1849 suggests that this marriage took place prior to European contact i
1792.

12 The people of Church House refer to themselves as "Homalco" tribe.

13 Johnny Chickite was the son of Jim Chickite. Jim was the elder brother of Joh
Dick, Sr. John Dick, Sr. changed his name to Dick after the name was given to hir
by workers at Hastings Mill in Vancouver who could not pronounce Chickite. Thi
was the way that a separate family line, the Dicks, was formed from the old Chick
ite family clan at Cape Mudge.

Notes to Chapter Two

1 In 1979–80, three bands of the Kwagiulth withdrew from the Kwakiutl Distric
Council to form the Mus-gamagw Tribal Council. The Nimpkish band at Aler
Bay, the largest in the district, is associated with the Mus-gamagw Tribal Council s
that together these four bands represent approximately 44 per cent of the whol
membership of the Kwagiulth bands. Though under different leadership, the tw
councils co-operate on a number of important functions such as education
fisheries resource management, and territorial claims.

2 The generalizing term "Kwakiutl," derived from the name of one of the tribe
based at Fort Rupert, has long been accepted by native and non-native people a
referring to all speakers of the Kwakwala language. This usage is reflected in th
title of a representative group, the Kwakiutl District Council. The museum at Cap
Mudge was titled "Kwakiutl" at the time of opening in 1979, but the spelling wa
later changed to Kwagiulth as a better rendering of the sound of this word. To ge
away from using the title of one band at Fort Rupert to stand for all bands of th
southern Kwagiulth, the word kwakwaka?wakw was proposed by the U'Mista Cul
tural Society at Alert Bay. It is coming into increasing use by scholars and nativ
speakers to the north, but is not in use in the Lekwiltok area. It means "speakers o
the Kwakwala language."

3 In his "Notes and Observations on the Kwakiool People" (1887), George M. Daw
son of the Geological Survey of Canada writes concerning the Lekwiltok: "Thes
tribes are closely allied, their central place being at Cape Mudge. They are togethe
known to the whites as the Li-kwil-tah or Uculta Indians. . . . They constitute th
southern branch of the Kwakiool people. . . . The Wi-we-eke constitute the premie

tribe of this group their village named Tsa-Kwa-loo-in and known to the whites as the 'Uculta Village' being situated on the west side of the Cape Mudge a short distance from its extremity."

4 Other divisions of the Lekwiltok have existed in the past, but these have disappeared as an entity and faded from memory of the Lekwiltok people. For reportage on the original groups constituting the Lekwiltok, see Franz Boas, *The Kwakiutl Indians*, Report of National Museum (1895), p. 331. See also Edward Curtis, *The North American Indian Vol. 10: The Kwakiutl* (1915), pp. 308–9. Marie Mauzé presents a complete documentation of the divisions of the Lekwiltok over time in her Ph.D. dissertation (in French), vol. 2 (Paris, 1984), pp. 384–409.

5 In 1914 the We-Wai-Kai, through their spokesman, Chief Billy Assu, requested that the village of Tekya be added to their allotment of reserves at a meeting of the Reserve Commission, who phrased this request as "the old village sites, the river and bay for its fishing, the mountain for its religious and historic association as the Kwawkewlth Ararat" (1916, 2:410). This request was refused by the Royal Commission in 1916.

6 The Awaetlala and Tanakteuk tribes of Knight Inlet shared the Klinaklini River with the Fort Rupert, Mamalilikulla, Tlawitsis, Matilpi, and Euclataw tribes for eulachon fishing and grease-making according to unpublished field notes ("Southern Kwakiutl," by Wilson Duff, c. 1960: courtesy, the Kwakiutl District Council). Klinaklini is a duplication of the Kwakwala word x̱ina meaning eulachon oil.

7 Ashdown Green, a representative of the provincial government, surveyed the reserves at Campbell River and Quinsam in 1888 after calling in at Cape Mudge to obtain guides, one of whom was Jim Naknakim.

8 According to recent research, the impact of the white man on the Indian populations along the Pacific coast resulted in a loss of two-thirds of the population (Kirk 1986: 225) This estimate of two-thirds holds true for the Kwagiulth people. The population decline for the whole Kwagiulth people, north and south, has been estimated as from about 10,700 in 1835, to a low of 1,854 by 1929 (Duff 1964: 39, table 3). The Kwagiulth people are a fast-growing population, and those registered in bands in the southern region, from Smith's Inlet south, now number over four thousand.

9 With the changes to the Indian Act of Canada, Bill C-31 (1985), numbers in the We-Wai-Kai band rose initially from 436 in 1985 to 496 in 1986. Numbers in the We-Wai-Kum band at Campbell River rose from 248 to 286 in the same period, and the Comox band went from 85 to 92. The Kwaikah residing at Campbell River with the We-Wai-Kum did not increase their number. By 23 March 1988, 576 were on the Cape Mudge Band list, increasing to 623 by February 1989; at which time the Lekwiltok tribe accounted for 1,102 of the Kwagiulth Nation.

Notes to Chapter Three

1 For more tales of events at the village of ǧʷiǧʷakulis, see Appendix 4.

2 In *The Coast Salish* (Barnett 1955: 25–26), the whale ritual is discussed in a context of close Lekwiltok-Comox relations in an area from Salmon River to Kye Bay, just north of the present village of Comox. George Mitchell, a Comox respondent, did not distinguish between the Lekwiltok and the Comox bands in the area. He regarded the Lekwiltok as one of the five highest ranking tribes of the group, who together were known as the "Whale House." Referring to these "ya yaqwiLtah," he makes the point that their personal family names were generally Kwakiutl. They were said to be located at Quathiaski Cove, but the context suggests Gowlland Harbour on Quadra Island.

   According to Mitchell, the five superior bands wintered at Cape Mudge and in the summer scattered to locations such as Salmon River, Rock Bay, Menzies Bay, and near Point Mudge. Collectively, they harassed the five other Comox groups in the area, one of which was the eiksa, who were in three locations around the mouth of the Campbell River.

Once a year the "Whale House" staged a whale ritual at which time "about twenty men used to enter a buoyant shell representing a whale. It was controlled by secret tow-lines and, as it bobbed up and down in the water of the bay, it was made to spout feathers."

3 A fuller version of what may be the same battle is found in Curtis (1915: 110–12). The Curtis version pits the Lekwiltok of Tekya against the Comox in the mouth of the Campbell River. The latter had been forced to move from their village on the river to a fortified position at "Qeqakulis" (Gowlland Harbour) to escape the wrath of the Lekwiltok, who had sought sanctuary with them from the mass attack of the southern allied tribes of Salish but had been betrayed by one man who welcomed them into his house but murdered each man as he came in.

According to an account given by Chief Billy Assu of Cape Mudge to R. Walker, the Lekwiltok who attacked the Comox fort on the cliffs in Gowlland Harbour spared the life of a Lekwiltok woman who was seated on a big basket, which she declared contained her belongings. Inside was her Comox husband, who thus escaped with his life (personal communication, Joy Huntley, née Walker, 1985). Since this singular episode is found both in Curtis and in local native history, it is probable that the battle described in these sources is the same, but the enemy of the Lekwiltok are said to be Haida in one version and Salish in another.

4 For circumstances surrounding two police actions taken by gunboat against the village of Cape Mudge, see Barry Gough, *Gunboat Frontier: British Maritime Authority and Northwest Coast Indians* (1984: 130–37).

5 Thunderbird is a supernatural being associated with thunder and lightning. As the great bird-spirit flies through the air, there are flashes of light, followed by the thunder of its wings. For a local history where Thunderbird plays a part, see Appendix 3.

6 In 1972, the We-Wai-Kai Band Council at Cape Mudge, concerned that the petroglyphs were in danger from erosion and vandalism, arranged to have seven of the finest examples of carved boulders brought in to the reserve at Cape Mudge where they are presently on display on the foreshore opposite the Kwagiulth Museum and beside the ramp leading into the museum.

Notes To Chapter Four

1 The reference is to a ritual, no longer performed, in which a war dancer dramatically calls into being awesome guardian spirit figures during the winter dance ceremonies. The effect of the spirits rising is achieved by pushing hinged vertical boards up from a concealed pit in the floor of the big house. As these pierced boards rise, section by section, they sway and tremble giving a life-like appearance to the sea-monsters. As well as these power boards representing sisiyuƛ, the giant deadly serpent in the sea, a huge horizontal representation of sisiyuƛ is said to have been raised up as well, in this instance.

2 Coppers are large shield-shaped plaques cut from copper ships' sheathing. They are painted with black lead, and a design representing some supernatural being, often in animal aspect, is brought out by removing the lead in the design area and allowing the copper to shine through. These coppers are considered very valuable and the price for them rises each time a copper is purchased until they have come to represent vast wealth. They have been exchanged at potlatches from the time of white contact until today. In the past they were often broken in rivalry potlatches where the destruction of wealth was an index of a chief's ability to best his rival. Billy Assu of Cape Mudge was the first of his people to acquire a copper (Drucker and Heizer 1967: 39–45). In an account of his many potlatches by Billy Assu, he

mentions the burning of his copper aisàma at a potlatch at Salmon River (Drucker, field notes, 1953.) See also Chapter 7, pp. 111–13, for a ceremony of the transfer of coppers at Harry Assu's potlatch of 1984.

3 This pole can be seen in a painting by Emily Carr entitled "Cape Mudge: An Indian Family with Totem Pole, 1912."

4 "Kwakiutl Indian Music of the Pacific Northwest," collected, recorded, and annotated by Dr. Ida Halpern (Ethnic Folkways Library, Album No. F.E. 4122, 1981).

5 Dr. Mark Skinner of Simon Fraser University reported to Heritage Conservation Branch, Victoria, on 5 February 1986 that a partial human skeleton of an adult native, dating from 2000 +/− 120 years before present was recovered from a large, stratified midden deposit at Cape Mudge Village, Quadra Island.

6 For the traditional story that accompanied the three potlatch figures when they were acquired at Cape Mudge, see Appendix 9.

Notes to Chapter Five

1 The relative numbers of fishermen of European, Japanese, and Indian origin had drastically changed from the early days of a preponderance of Indians fishing. "In former times nearly the entire work at the canneries was, with the exception of a few Chinese employees, monopolized by the Indians; but the advent of the Japanese and others in later years, has to some extent lessened the earnings of those Indians engaged in the prosecution of that Industry" (Canada, *Annual Report on Indian Affairs 1895:* p. 168).

"The success of the Kwakiutl in adjusting to the new economic conditions can be set in clearer relief by considering the size and character of the labour force with which they compete. The total population of British Columbia in 1931 was somewhat less than 700,000. Included in this figure were more than 45,000 Chinese and slightly more than 22,000 Japanese. The Kwakiutl at this time numbered slightly over 1,000" (Codere 1950: 41)

2 Results of Dr. Peter H. Pearse's investigations are published in *Turning the Tide: A New Policy for Canada's Pacific Fisheries* (Ottawa: Department of Fisheries and Oceans, September 1982).

3 In 1974, Judge George Bolt ruled that the Indians of the state of Washington were entitled to take up to half of the salmon and steelhead trout runs, based on the 1855 tribal treaty right to fish at traditional fishing grounds off the reservation.

Notes to Chapter Seven

1 For the circumstances surrounding the potlatch suppression and its effects on the native people in the Kwagiulth area with evidence from native people involved in the proceedings of that time, see *Prosecution or Persecution* by Daisy (My-yah-nelth) Sewid-Smith (1979). For confiscation and return of Kwagiulth potlatch gear as part of an international trend to repatriation, see "Cultural Readjustment, a Canadian Case Study" by Stephen Inglis in *Gazette: Quarterly of the Canadian Museums Association* 12 (Summer 1979). See also, "The Potlatch Law and the Confiscation of Ceremonial Property among the Kwakiutl" by Marie Mauzé, *Bulletin Amérique Indienne* (July 1983), translated by Katherine Odgers, Kwagiulth Museum, Cape Mudge.

2 George M. Heye, founder and collector for the Museum of the American Indian, Heye Foundation, New York.

3 The Spirit of Dancing, referred to as "Klassila," had been imprisoned in Ottawa for many years and was now being released to the Kwagiulth people. The Power of the Spirit was symbolically thrown from ship to shore, where it was "caught" and set the catcher dancing. He in turn hurled the spirit across the beach and through

the museum doors. The spirit had entered the ceremonial house (museum).

4 The dances in the Red Cedar Bark series are said to be "serious" because they portray the suffering of the men and women who endured the struggle against death on the extended spirit quests once undertaken by the young initiates into the dancing societies of the Northwest Coast. Some dances depict this anguish of mind and body that was experienced in encounters with the supernaturals. Then life itself was at risk from devouring monsters or by drowning, fire, or war. It was the "dark side of life" that must be gone through to achieve full adult status. Its reenactment could involve ritual torture. The relationship between tribal masks and exorcism of the fear of death has been pointed out by M. M. Halpin, MOA, *Museum Note* 18 (n.d.).

5 See Appendix 7 for "Lament of the Nobles," translated by Daisy Sewid-Smith and published in *Campbell River Salmon Festival Souvenir Booklet* (1973).

6 An explanation of "coppers" has been given in note 2, Chapter 4.

7 The events of this potlatch were video-taped and may be seen by arrangement with the Kwagiulth Museum, Cape Mudge.

8 bǝxbǝxʷǝlanusiwe is the cannibal monster whose name is translated as "Cannibal-at-the-north-end-of-the-world." His body is covered with dreadful mouths that emit a whistling sound. He desires human flesh to eat and is seeking it out. The supernatural birds – Hox Hox, Crooked Beak, and Raven – secure the food for bǝxbǝxʷǝlanusiwe. The hamatsa dancer portrays a hunter who encountered the monster and his terrible attendants and returns to his home community in a state of frenzy with the power of the cannibal still upon him. It should be noted that cannibalism was so abhorrent to the Coastal Indian people that it clearly indicated a seizure by an inhuman and supernatural agency.

A Kwagiulth version of the myth of the Cannibal-at-the-north-end-of the world, he who feasts himself upon the tribes but is outwitted by the brave hamatsas, is told by George Hunt for Franz Boas in *Thirty-fifth Annual Report of the Bureau of American Ethnology*, Part 2, Smithsonian Institution (Washington, D.C., 1921), pp. 1222–48.

For a complete account of the story that animates this ritual Hamatsa Dance, see Curtis (1915), 10: 165–70.

For definitive information on the traditional enactment of the Hamatsa ritual see Audrey Hawthorn, *Kwakiutl Art* (1979), pp. 45, 46.

For photo illustration and explanation of the contemporary dances of the Kwagiulth including the myth of bǝxbǝxʷǝlanusiwe, see Peter L. Macnair "Kwakiutl Winter Dances: A Reenactment" (Toronto: Artscanada, 1977), pp. 62–86.

See also "The Origin of the Hamat'sa," a clear account of the cannibal monster myth from the Indians of the Rivers Inlet, a region from which the Kwagiulth got this and many other of their dances. *Yaxwattan's. Learning Kwakwala Series. Book 12* by Jay Powell, Vickie Jensen, Vera Cranmer, and Agnes Cranmer. (Alert Bay U'Mista Society, n.d.).

9 Animals shown in the performances are not common forest animals but representations of supernatural beings that can transform from aspects of other animals to human form and back again. This distinction is indicated here by capitalizing the names, for example, Raven, Bear, and Wolf. In the time prior to the transformation of earth to its present form, all animals, including man, lived in similar social arrangements with chiefs, houses, and treasures. Occasionally, a young person seeking spirit power would encounter a supernatural being who would remove scales, feathers, or fur and reveal his human aspect in order to communicate with the suppliant and grant that person some treasure such as hunting prowess. Seekers were provided with symbols of their newly acquired status: name, song, costume, or mask. It is the story of these encounters that families show in the potlatch to validate the crests, dances, and songs that they have acquired the right to show.

Appendices

1 *Linguistic Key to the Orthography* by Peter Wilson.

2 *Kʷakʷala Words* by Peter Wilson.

3 *How the Lekwiltok Obtained Eulachon Fishing Rights on Knight Inlet*, by Franz Boas.

4 Qā'teᵋnats *and* Qā'teᵋmo, a Lekwiltok tale. Franz Boas and George Hunt.

5 *Two versions of the Acquisition of the* kwéxwe *dance by Wai-Kai from the Supernatural Red Cods*. Franz Boas and George Hunt.

6 *Most Beautiful One*, excerpts from a We-Wai-Kum tale.

7 *Lament of the Nobles*, a mourning song sung at potlatches to honour the departed. Daisy Sewid-Smith by permission of James Sewid.

8 *The Welcome Pole*, a story associated with the right to display these poles. Kwagiulth Museum, Cape Mudge.

9 *Descendants of Ida and Harry Assu*.

10 *Duntsik Board from Cape Mudge*, describing the use of these boards in traditional spirit dancing. Kwagiulth Museum, Cape Mudge.

Appendix 1

Linguistic Key to the Orthography
Peter Wilson

There are forty-eight sounds in the Kwakwala language. In this book, the orthography chosen to represent these sounds employs one symbol for each sound. These symbols are based on the guidelines of the International Phonetic Association and are used widely among Northwest Coast writers, educators, linguists, and anthropologists. This writing system is also used in schools where the language is studied.

Kwakwala speakers use a variety of sounds not found in English. Two specific groups of sounds warrant some preliminary description. First, a large number of consonants are pronounced with accompanying glottal closure, making them sound emphasized. These sounds are represented by a raised comma, e.g. /p̓/. Second, there are those sounds whose primary point of articulation occurs in the back velar area, i.e., the back of the tongue touches the back roof of the mouth, e.g., /ǧ/. To the untrained ear, these sounds are often mistaken for similar sounds which occur in English, e.g., /g/.

Kwakwala to English Sound Correspondence Approximation

a	"a" as in "father"
b	"b" as in "big"
c	similar to "ts" in "cats"
c̓	glottalized "ts" sound
d	"d" as in "dig"
dᶻ	"d" and "z" pronounced together "dz"
e	similar to "ea" in "great"
ə	similar to "u" in "but"
g	"g" and "y" pronounced together "gy"
gʷ	"g" and "w" pronounced together "gw"
ǧ	similar to "g" pronounced in back of mouth
ǧʷ	similar to "gw" pronounced in back of mouth
h	"h" as in "hat"
i	similar to "ee" in "meet"
ḵ	"k" and "y" pronounced together "ky"
k̓	glottalized "ky" sound
ḵʷ	"k" and "w" pronounced together "kw"
k̓ʷ	glottalized "kw" sound
ḷ	"l" as in "left"
l	glottalized "l" sound
ł	voiceless "l" sound
λ	similar to "gl" in "glue"
ƛ	similar to "cl" in "clue"
ƛ̓	glottalized "cl" as in "clue"
m	"m" as in "moon"
m̓	glottalized "m" sound
n	"n" as in "noon"
n̓	glottalized "n" sound
o	similar to "oa" in "boat"
p	"p" as in "pipe"
p̓	glottalized "p" sound
q	similar to "k" sound pronounced in back of mouth
q̓	glottalized "k" sound pronounced in back of mouth
qʷ	similar to "k" and "w" as "kw" pronounced in back of mouth
q̓ʷ	glottalized "kw" pronounced in back of mouth

s	"s" as in "snake"
t	"t" as in "tip"
t̓	glottalized "t" sound
u	similar to "oo" in "boot"
w	"w" as in "wide"
ẇ	glottalized "w" sound
x	similar to "ky" but continuous
x^w	similar to "kw" but continuous
x̌	back "k" /q/ but continuous
x̌^w	back "kw" /q / but continuous
y	"y" as in "yes"
ẏ	glottalized "y" sound
ʔ	glottal stop, similar to pause between syllables in "uh-uh"

Other orthographies are also in use in the Kwagiulth area. A practical orthography using the letters of the English alphabet was devised in the 1970's by Randy Bouchard and put into use in various Indian communities. This system was adapted to Kwakwala by David Grubb in 1972 and explained in *A Practical Writing System and Short Dictionary of Kwakw'ala (Kwakiutl)*, National Museum of Man, Ottawa, Service Paper No. 34.

The U'Mista Cultural Society in Alert Bay later prepared a cultural program utilizing Kʷakʷʔala language materials in another practical orthography (incidentally related to the Bouchard-Grubb system).

Appendix 2

kʷak̓ʷala Words

This appendix gives an alphabetized list of the kʷak̓ʷala words used in the book. Eac[h] entry contains a transcription of the word based on pronunciations given by Harr[y] Assu. The transcriptions, therefore, represent the liq̓ʷala dialect of kʷak̓ʷala that [is] spoken by Harry Assu.

The kʷak̓ʷala words written in the text preserve the original spelling and writing con[-] ventions of their sources. This leads to two difficulties: first, many of the sources us[e] different writing systems; and second, many of the publications cited have not tran[-] scribed the language accurately. The list of kʷak̓ʷala words presented here serves to co[r-] rect this problem and to assist the reader who may be unfamiliar with some of th[e] terms used.

The alphabetic order used in this appendix is based on English order (i.e. a, [b,] c,...). Non-English symbols are located to their closest English equivalent. The ord[er] is listed below:

a b c ć d dᶻ e ə g gʷ ǧ ǧʷ h i k kʷ k̓ k̓ʷ l ƚ ł λ
x̌ m m̓ n n̓ o p p̓ q qʷ q̓ q̓ʷ s t t' u w w̓ x xʷ x̌ x̌ʷ
y̓
(The symbol ? "glottal stop" is ignored in the ordering of the symbols)

For example, [kʷ] "rounded k" is found following [k]. The vowel [ə] "schwa," which looks like an upside down [e], is found following [e]. The letters [λ], [x̌], an[d] [x̌] (based on "lambda" are found following the other [l] letters.

Each entry consists of three or more parts. The first word given in an entry is alway[s] the word written exactly as it is found in the text.

The following word is the translation "eagle." Following the translation is an ab[-] breviation for the source of this word. For example: kʷikʷ eagle (nw) In this exampl[e] the word is listed with (nw), which stands for Standard Northwest Transcription. Th[is] source means that Harry Assu has pronounced the word and that it has been tran[-] scribed into the Standard Northwest Transcription.

Other entries contain more information. Where words occur in the text that are n[ot] written in the Standard Northwest Transcription, an additional entry follows the boo[k] entry in square brackets. This entry is the same word transcribed into the Standar[d] Northwest Transcription. For example: Gwayee [gʷay̓i] Village in Kingcome Inl[et] (inac) The first word "Gwayee" is the form of the word written in the text. The for[m] [gʷay̓i] is the same word written in the Standard Northwest Transcription. The transl[a-] tion "Village in Kingcome Inlet" follows. This source (inac) stands for "Indian an[d] Northern Affairs Canada."

One other section is contained in some entries. Following the translation of som[e] words is a "literal" translation. It normally occurs with names of people or places. Fo[r] example: gʷaǧəmlis is the word in kʷak̓ʷala used for Duncan Bay. It means "bay facin[g] north." The literal translations are enclosed in single quotes. Where a word in kʷak̓ʷa[la] has more than one meaning in English, the translations are separated by a semi-colo[n] as illustrated below: ʔum̓alaƚ noble lady; princess (nw)

Abbreviations

inac Indian and Northern Affairs Canada. 1987.
nw Northwest Standard Transcription Words pronounced by Harry Assu in the liq̓ʷala dialect.
bar Homer Barnett. *The Coast Salish*. 1955.
dr Drucker. "Field Notes." 1953.
wd Wilson Duff. Unpublished field notes. (c. 1960)
su Source Unknown
com Spelling is in common use in English or in legal documents.
kdc Kwakiutl District Council
cur E.S. Curtis. *The North American Indian*. Vol. 10, 1915.
kg Franz Boas. *Kwakiutl Grammar*. 1947.
gd George Dawson. "Notes and Observations of the Kwakiool People." 1887.
ems E.M. Skinner. "Plan of the Laich-Kwil-Tach Indian Reserves." May 18, 1889.
fbl Franz Boas. *Part 2, Thirty-fifth Annual Report of the Bureau of American Ethnology*, Smithsonian Institution. New York. 1921.
rcl Royal Commissions 1. 1915.

a

ʔaʔumalał a dance shown in the potlatch (nw)
Abayah [ʔabayaʔa] wife of Mungo Martin (com)
aisā'ma Name of a copper (dr)
ʔax̌igalis area in Campbell River near Lane Field (nw)
Awaetlala [ʔaẃix̌əla] Tribe originally from Knight Inlet (wd)

b

bagʷani Name; Chief from Alert Bay (nw)
bəgʷis Man-of-the-Sea 'sea man' (nw)
bə̄xbəxʷəlanusiwe cannibal monster (nw)

c

całcəx̌isa Village at Drew Harbour (nw)
Cukwakileese [gəldədᶻulis] Village on Nimpkish River 'big long beach, long flat beach' (com)

c̓

c̓akʷalotən present Village at Cape Mudge; abandoned Salish Village at Point Mudge (also pronounced as c̓akʷaluʔtən) (nw) (alternate spelling c̓akʷaloten [com])
c̓eʔqa winter dance; dark side of life as enacted at potlatch rituals (nw)
c̓əlǧʷadi Village near Port Hardy 'place of warmth' (nw)

d dᶻ

dəxdəxəlił owl (nw)
dᶻax̌ʷən eulachon fish (nw)
dᶻunuq̓ʷa wild man/woman of the woods (nw)

e

eiksan a Comox Tribe once located on the Campbell River (bar)
Euclataw [liǧʷiłdaʔx̌ʷ] Tribe from Cape Mudge/Campbell River (com)

ʔewanuk^w Harry Assu 'watching the point' (nw)

ə

ənqalis Steve Assu 'opening the mouth for food' (nw)
ʔənq^wəla Name of a copper 'foggy' (nw)

g　g^w

Gakula [gax̌iƛağəm] Gakula masks introduced in the Klassila ceremony (com)
Galgome [galǧ^wəmi] Johnny Galgome (com)
gəldəd^zulis Village on Nimpkish River 'big long beach, long flat beach' (nw)
giǧəme chief (nw)
Gildees [gəldis] Gildees (name of H.A.'s gill-netter) 'big long beach, long flat beach' (com)
gix̌^ws̩əm a band subdivision of the [weweq̓eʔ] 'chiefs' (nw)
Gwa'sala [g^waʔsəla] Tribe originally from Smith's Inlet (inac)
Gway-as-dums [g^waẏasdəms] Village on Gilford Island (inac)
Gwayee [g^waẏi] Village in Kingcome Inlet (inac)
g^wanusbaʔ Quathiaski Cove 'place on north side of point' (nw)
g^waǧəmlis Duncan Bay 'bay facing north' (nw)

ǧ　ǧ^w

ǧaluq^wəmɬ a Hamatsa bird dance 'crooked beak' shown at potlatch (nw)
ǧ^waẇino raven (nw)
ǧ^wəẏəm whale (nw)
ǧ^wiǧ^wakulis Village at Gowlland Harbour (nw)

h

Haisla [x̌aʔisala] Tribe from Kitimat area; Haisla Tribe; Language of Haisla Tribe (com)
Hakuweela Name (su)
Hamatsa [hamaća] Hamatsa; a ritual performance; one who dances the Hamatsa ritual; a ritual society; a member of the Hamatsa ritual society; a cannibal ritual performance (com)

Hamaća [hamaća] Hamatsa; a ritual performance; one who dances the Hamatsa ritual; a ritual society; a member of the Hamatsa ritual society; a cannibal ritual performance (com)
hamatsas [hamacas] members of the society of Hamatsa (i.e. cannibal) dancers (fb1)
Heiltsuk [heɬd^zaq^w] Tribe from Bella Bella (com)
helagal'is a raven dancer (nw)
heligaʔ Potlatch attendant, Hamatsa leader, female relation of Hamatsa dancer who pacifies Hamatsa (nw)
heɬatusa Name; Transformer spirit 'correct, right' (nw)
həmd^zid father of George Dick (nw)
həmsəmɬ bird monsters of Hamatsa ritual (nw)
həmx̌^wəmax̌aʔas a cliff in Gowlland Harbour 'jumping down place' (nw)
holikəlaɬ leader of Klassila ritual (nw)
HOMAY-NO HOMAY-NO Reserve No. 2 (com)
Homalco [x̌^wəmaɬku] Tribe from Church House (com)
hux̌^whuq^w a type of ceremonial bird monster mask; a bird monster dance that is part of the Hamatsa ritual; bird monster crest (nw)
hwulk [x̌^wəlk^w] Village of the Nimpkish Tribe on the Nimpkish River (su)

i

ʔisəməla Name of a copper 'abalone face' (nw)

k　k^w

Kanish [qañis] Kanish Bay (on Quadra Island) (com)
kəmqolas Charley Assu, father of Billy Assu (nw)
Klahuse [ƛəx̌us] Tribe from Squirrel Cove (su)
Klakwatsi [ƛaq̓^wad^zi] Johnny Klakwatsi 'big copper' (com)

Klassila [ƛaʔsala] a potlatch dance ceremony (com)

Klinaklini [ƛinaƛina] Klinaklini River. This word is a reduplication of the word [ƛina] which means 'eulachon oil.' (com)

Kuloose [qulus] a supernatural bird, younger brother of thunderbird (com)

Kwa-wa-aineuk [gʷawaʔenux̌ʷ] Tribe from Drury Inlet, at Hopetown-Watson Island (kdc)

Kwakiutl [kʷagoʔɬ] Tribe from Fort Rupert; generic name for the Kwakwala-speaking people who inhabit the region from Campbell River/Cape Mudge in the south to Smith Inlet in the north (kdc)

Other spellings of the name are listed below:
  Kwakiool (gd)
  Kwagiulth (kdc)
  Kwawkewlth (rcl)
  kʷagoʔɬ (nw)
  kʷaguɬ (nw) (alternate pronunciation)

Kwaikah [k̓ʷix̌a] Tribe from Phillips Arm (com)

Kwakwaka'wakw [kʷakʷakawakʷ] Speakers of Kwakwala language (com)

Kwakwala [kʷakʷala] Language of Tribe from Fort Rupert and the Kwakwala-speaking people who inhabit the region from Campbell River/Cape Mudge in the south to Smith Inlet on the north (com)

Kwicksutaineuk [qʷiqʷ̩sutinux̌ʷ] Tribe from Gilford Island (ĸdc)

Kwieksutaineuk [qʷiqʷəsutinux̌ʷ] Tribe from Gilford Island (inac)

Kwiksutaineuk [qʷiqʷəsutinux̌ʷ] Tribe from Gilford Island (com)

Kwē'xwe [x̌ʷex̌ʷe] a ritual dance performance (fb1)

Kʷakʷala [kʷakʷala] Language of the Tribe from Fort Rupert and the Kwakwala-speaking people who inhabit the region from Campbell River/Cape Mudge in the south to Smith Inlet in the north (com)

kʷagoʔɬ Tribe from Fort Rupert; generic name for the Kwakwala-speaking people who inhabit the region from Campbell River/Cape Mudge in the south to Smith Inlet in the north (nw)

kʷakum Kwakume Inlet (nw)

kʷaxsistala Quocksister, a family name (nw)

kʷakʷala Language of the Tribe from Fort Rupert and the Kwakwala-speaking people who inhabit the region from Campbell River/Cape Mudge in the south to Smith Inlet in the north (com)

kʷənkʷənxʷəlige thunderbird (nw)

kʷənsəm Reserve on Quinsam River; community on Quinsam Reserve; area along Quinsam River (nw)

kʷənxʷaʔuǧʷa a wife of Billy Assu and widow of Johnny Moon (m. 1926 to Billy Assu) 'thunder woman' (nw)

kʷikʷ eagle (nw)

k̓ k̓ʷ

k̓awas thin smoked dried salmon (nw)

k̓ʷix̌a Tribe from Phillips Arm/Campbell River (nw)

l

Lekwiltok [liǧʷiɬdaʔx̌ʷ] Tribe from Cape Mudge/Campbell River region (com)

Other spellings are listed below:
  Laich-Kwil-Tach (ems)
  Legwiɬdaʔx̌ʷ (nw)
  lekwiltik (dr)
  Li-kwil-tah (gd)
  liǧʷiɬdaʔx̌ʷ (nw)
  Uculta (gd)
  Yaculta (com)
  Yukwiɬ'tək (dr)

ləgwiʔɬ [ləǧʷiʔɬ] fire of the house 'fire in house' (kg)

liq̓ʷala Language of Cape Mudge/Campbell River people (nw)

lix̌ᵈᶻaq̓ʷala [lix̌ᵈᶻaq̓ʷala] Language of Cape Mudge/Campbell River (nw)

lubiɬila name of a copper 'every cent went into buying it' (nw)

Lōkwola a copper (dr)

ɬ λ ƛ ƛ̓

ƛaʔamin Tribe from Powell River (nw)

ɬədis Island in Campbell River (nw)

ƛugʷe gift to a family from supernatural 'treasure' (nw)

ƛaʔsala a potlatch dance ceremony (nw)

ƛalap̓eniǧa wife of Charlie Assu, paternal grandmother of Harry Assu (nw)

ƛam̓atəxʷ Village located on Campbell River Estuary (nw)

ƛəliliƛa Don Assu 'always inviting' (also ƛiʔɬəla) (nw)

ƛixƛəx̌ilkʷ a house in Village Island 'sea lion house' (nw)

ƛ̓eq̓ʷala Ceremonial ending of the mourning period of the Potlatch 'to shake off sorrows' (nw)

ƛ̓inaƛ̓ina [ƛ̓inaƛ̓ina] Klinaklini River 'ƛ̓ina' = eulachon oil said twice (nw)

ƛ̓ina eulachon oil (nw)

m

MA-TSAY-NO [nəc̓inux̌ʷ] Tribe from Phillips Arm; MA-TSAY-NO (com)

makmusa Jim Wallace (nw)

Mamalelequala [mamaliliqəla] Tribe from Village Island (inac)

Mamalilikulla [mamaliliqəla] Tribe from Village Island (com)

maməliliqəla Tribe from Village Island (nw)

Maquilla [mək̓ʷəla] Johnny Moon 'moon' (su)

MAT-LA-TEN [məƛətən] MAT-LA-TEN Reserve No. 4 (com)

Matilpi [madiɬbaʔ] Tribe group from Village Island (com)

məʔdəm a dance shown in potlatch (nw)

məƛ̓ənac Mitlenatch Island (nw)

Mitlenatch [məƛ̓ənac] Mitlenatch Island (com)

Mitlenatch Island [məƛ̓ənac] Mitlenatch Island (com)

Mus-gamagw [musǧamak̓ʷ] Mus-gamagw Tribal Council 'four tribes' (com)

m̓

m̓al'ap name of a canoe 'white bottom' (nw)

m̓axʷaʔuǧʷa Mary Naknakim 'great potlatch giver woman' (nw)

m̓axʷaʔuǧʷa Name; mother of Harry Assu 'great potlatch giver woman' (nw)

m̓axʷaʔuǧʷa Colleen Dick 'great potlatch giver woman' (nw)

m̓ək̓ʷəla Johnny Moon 'moon' (nw)

m̓əlm̓adᶻu thin smoked dried halibut (nw)

n

Naknakim [n̓axn̓agəm] grandfather of Billy Assu 'from daylight to daylight' (com)

nəgedᶻi Billy Assu 'big mountain' (nw)

nəqaʔbənkəm Mungo Martin (nw)

Nimpkish [n̓əmǧis] Tribe from Alert Bay (com)

Nu'tsi Lekwiltok [noc̓a] Name of a man called Dr. Powell (who was also known as the strong man from Cape Mudge) (cur)

nuɬəmaɬa fool dance, part of Hamatsa ritual (nw)

Nuyumbalees [nuyəmbalis] Society operating museum in Cape Mudge 'the beginning of all legends' (com)

n̓

'Nakwaxda'xw [n̓ak̓ʷaxdaʔx̌ʷ] Tribe originally from Blunden Harbour (inac)

n̓am̓ima a band sub-group (extended family) (nw)

n̓əmǧis Tribe from Alert Bay (nw)

n̓ən̓alaɬ dance shown at a potlatch 'day dance' (nw)

o

Oweekeeno [ʔəwikinux̌ʷ] Tribe from Rivers Inlet (com)

ʔoyaca Jim Naknakim 'grandfather' (nw)

ozistal'is [ʔodᶻistal'is] Billy Assu; Dan Assu (nw)

p

pedʔᶻədᶻiyəm Name (Fitzgerald) (nw)

pəlpaqoḷis Middle Point 'in the middle' (in middle of Menzies Bay) (nw)

pəx̌əla shaman (nw)

potlamin [paʔɬamin] Mt. Estero (com)

ṗ

ṗaʔsəlaɫ Billy Assu 'gives potlatches' (nw)
ṗadᶻiyus Tom Wallace 'high river' (also pronounced as ṗadᶻolis) (nw)
ṗəsa to potlatch (nw)
ṗəsala Billy Assu 'potlatcher' (nw)

q qʷ

qaṅis Kanish Bay (nw)
qaẇicən old native village behind Yellow Island (nw)
Qeqakulis [ǧʷiǧʷakulis] Village in Gowlland Harbour (cur)
Quak-sis-ta [kʷaxsistala] Quak-sis-ta; a family name (su)
Quatsino [gʷaċinux̌ʷ] Tribe originally from Koprino Harbour (kdc)
Quatsino [ǧusgimuxʷ] Tribe from Coal Harbour (com)
Quawselah [gʷaʔsəla] Tribe originally from Smith Inlet (inac)
QUIN-SAM [kʷənsəm] Quinsam Reserve No. 12 (com)
quluma Name of H. Assu's copper (from J. Sewid) (nw)
qulus a supernatural bird, younger bro. of thunderbird (nw)
Quocksister [kʷaxsistala] Quocksister; a family name (com)
Qwe'Qwa'Sot'Enox [qʷiqʷəsutinux̌ʷ] Tribe from Gilford Island (inac)
qʷiqʷəsutinux̌ʷ Tribe from Gilford Island (nw)

q̇ q̇ʷ

q̇asa crying (nw)
q̇ehwuqʔanux a woman's name (dr)
q̇exƛalaǧa Joy Inglis 'lots of fire' (nw)
q̇uminəwaǧas a dance shown in the potlatch (nw)
q̇umuksa Tribe from Comox (nw)

s

SA-AI-YOUCK [saʔeẏəkʷ] SA-AI-YOUCK Reserve No. 6 (com)
Saiiyouk [saʔeẏəkʷ] Village near mouth of Bute Inlet (com)

sisiyuƛ sea monster (nw)
Siwis [siwis] father of John Dick Sr. 'noted man' (nw)
suṗid presentation of a potlatch gift that is at once redeemed 'pass on' (nw)

t

Takush [tagʷis] Village in Smith Inlet (kdc)
Tekya [təka] Village in Topaze Harbour 'dirt, soil, earth' (com)
Tenaktak (daṅaxdaʔx̌ʷ) Tribe from Knight Inlet (com)
Tlawitsis [ɬawiċis] Tribe from Turnour Island (com)
Tokwit [tuʔxʷid] a dance shown in the potlatch; lady dancer with magical powers (com)
Tsa-Kwa-loo-in [ċakʷalotən] present Village at Cape Mudge; abandoned Salish Village at Point Mudge (also pronounced as ċakʷaluʔtən) (gd)
Tsquloten [ċakʷalotən] present Village at Cape Mudge; abandoned Salish Village at Point Mudge (also pronounced as ċakʷaluʔtən) (com)
Tsulquata [ċəlǧʷadi] Village in Port Hardy 'place of warmth' (inac)
tuʔxʷid a dance shown in the potlatch; lady dancer with magical powers (also pronounced as tuxʷʔid) (nw)
Twawataineuk [dᶻawadeʔenux̌ʷ] Tribe from Kingcome Inlet (inac)

ṫ

ṫaʔqay Deepwater Bay (nw)
ṫatapaʔulis Whiterock Pass (nw)
ṫəka Village in Topaze Harbour 'soil, dirt, earth' (nw)
ṫətapaʔulis Village at White Rock Pass (nw)

u

ʔuʔstoy Seymour Narrows at site of Ripple Rock (nw)
Uculta [liǧʷiɫdaʔx̌ʷ] Tribe from Cape Mudge/Campbell River (gd)
ʔuɫ Menzies Bay 'big bay' (nw)

U'Mista [ʔuṁista] U'Mista Cultural Society at Alert Bay (com)

ʔuṁalał noble lady; princess (nw)

ʔuniqʷa a dance shown in the potlatch (nw)

w

waʔq̓es frog (also pronounced as wəq̓es) (nw)

Wai-Kai [weqaʔi] Name of Ancestral Chief (com) also spelled as:
    We-Kai (su)
    weqaʔi (nw)
    wīqe (dr)

Walitsum [ẇalacaṁa] Tribe originally from Salmon River (com)

Walkus [wakas] a family name (com)

Wamish [waṁis] uncle of Billy Assu and brother of Charley Assu 'people going to dry fish on beach by river' (nw)

weʔdᶻulis a type of cloud cover (herring season) (nw)

We-Kai [weqaʔi] Name of Ancestral Chief (su)

We-Wai-Kai [weweq̓eʔ] Band from Cape Mudge (also pronounced as wiweq̓eʔ) (eng)
also spelled as:
    Wewayaka (su)
    weweq̓eʔ (nw)
    wiweq̓eʔ (nw)

We-Wai-Kum [weweq̓əm] Band from Campbell River (also pronounced as wiweq̓əm) (com)

weqaʔi Name of Ancestral Chief (nw)

Wewaikum [weweqəm] Band from Campbell River (also pronounced as wiweq̓əm) (com)

Wewayakay [weweq̓ʔ] Band from Cape Mudge (also pronounced as wiweq̓eʔ) (su)

weweq̓eʔ Band from Cape Mudge (also pronounced as wiweq̓eʔ) (com)

weweq̓əm Band from Campbell River (also pronounced as wiweq̓əm) (com)

wəndᶻisbalis sea monster near Cape Mudge (nw)

Whulk [x̌ʷəlkʷ] Village of the Nimpkish Tribe on the Nimpkish River (com)

wiweqeʔ Band from Cape Mudge (also pronounced as weweqeʔ see above) (nw)

Wulásu Name of chief from Gilford Island (dr)

wīqe [weqaʔi] Name of Ancestral Chief (dr)

w̄

w̄alacaṁa Band from Salmon River (nw)

x   xʷ

xʷisa marriage (nw)

x̌   x̌ʷ

x̌aʔisala Haisla Tribe, Name of canoe (nw)

x̌aṅaǧəmaẏa Harry Assu 'top giver' (nw)

x̌ʷax̌ʷəlǧʷaʔas Dogfish Bay 'place of the dogfish' (nw)

x̌ʷətis Old Quatsino Village (kdc)

x̌ʷix̌ʷi a dance shown in the potlatch, a dancer who dances the [x̌ʷix̌ʷi] dance (nw)

y

Yaculta [liǧʷiłdaʔx̌ʷ] Tribe from Cape Mudge/Campbell River (com)

yaqusəlagəlis Nicole Assu (nw)

yawenoo-k [yaw̄inox̌ʷ] daughter of Charley Assu (su)

yaxwatłanʔs Book Title 'We Will Dance' (su)

yax̌nəkʷaʔas Billy Assu 'can give thing away' (nw)

yax̌nəkʷaʔas Harry Assu 'can give thing away' (nw)

yayaqwiltak One of the tribes in the Whale House confederacy (bar)

yəqiλəsṁe father-in-law of Harry Mountain (nw)

Yukwiłtok [liǧʷiłdaʔx̌ʷ] Tribe from Cape Mudge/Campbell River (com)

Appendix 3

How the Lekwiltok Obtained Eulachon Fishing Rights on Knight Inlet

He asked his mother: "What is swimming in the river here? It looks like worms." She replied: "Those are oulachons. They are fat. Make a trap at the point on the bench where the drift of logs are and make a string of grass and try to fish."

Then he went back to the river and saw a canoe coming. It stopped on the beach in the same place where B'ā′Lalag·ilakᵘ was sitting. Wē′qaē was in the canoe. He spoke: "What are you doing at my river?" B'ā′Lalag·ilakᵘ replied: "Is that your river? Then tell me what kinds of fish go up the river?" Wē′qaē said: "These are the kinds of fish that go up my river: Steel head salmon, spring salmon, silver salmon, dog salmon, humpback salmon, trouts, that is all." Then B'ā′Lalag·ilakᵘ replied: "Is that all that goes up the river?" Wē′qaē said: "That is all." But B'ā′Lalag·ilakᵘ added: "Oulachon go up my river." "Oh, I forgot that. Let us go ashore. I want to take that boy into my canoe," said Wē′qaē. B'ā′Lalag·ilakᵘ asked his sisters to stay where they were. He was taken and tied in Wē′qaē's canoe. He made him a slave. Now they went down the inlet and came to Dōx′nalits'ē′naē. Then B'ā′Lalag·ilakᵘ moved in the canoe and flew away. In vain they tried to catch him with their paddles. He flew home. Wē′qaē traveled on and came to Qā′qetEn. There he saw the thunder bird sitting on a rock. He landed under the mountain where the thunder bird was sitting, but he did not go out of his canoe. Then the thunder bird sent the wind maker to hear what they said. He went down and heard Wē′qaē saying: "I thought he always made it hail." Then the wind maker went back to tell the thunder bird what he had heard. Now the thunder bird arose and went into his house. He put on his eagle dress and came out again. Right away there was thunder and lightning and a hail storm and a gale was blowing in Ts'awatē. Then Wē′qaē was blown up the inlet. In this manner the Lekwiltoq obtained the oulachon.

Franz Boas, *The Social Organization and Secret Societies of the Kwakiutl Indians* (1897), pp. 417–18.

Appendix 4

Qā′teᵋnats and Qā′teᵋmo. A tale of struggle for power between a young shaman and an older shaman at Tsquloten, a village on the cliffs at Cape Mudge near Mitlenatch Island

Listen, and I will tell you the story of the first of the Lē′gwiłdaᵋxᵘ, who lived in a village at the place named Tilted-Ground. Qāteᵋmo was a great shaman. He always cured the sick ones, and he was paid with slaves, canoes, and princesses of the chiefs. Therefore Qā′teᵋmo was a real chief, and Qā′teᵋnats was jealous of him. Qā′teᵋnats wished to purify himself in the river, and he asked his younger brother to go with him and purify himself in the river. They started to go to the river at the end of the village site. Qā′teᵋnats and his younger brother started and went to the upper part of the river. They saw a rock in the river, and on it lay some bark. Then Qā′teᵋnats asked his younger brother to purify himself farther down the river. Qā′teᵋnats did not wish to be near his younger brother while he was purifying himself. Every morning and every evening they went. Now they had purified for four days, but then in the evening they went to purify again, and sat on the rock on which the piece of bark was. Then they heard something moving in the salal-bushes, and Qā′teᵋnats was frightened. Therefore he broke a piece of the bark and threw it at the thing that made the sound in the salal bushes. Then the noise that they had heard ceased. As soon as they had finished purifying, Qā′teᵋnats went home and lay down in his bedroom with his younger brother. It was not yet daylight (in the morning) when Qā′teᵋnats woke his younger brother. His younger brother arose at once, and they went out of the house to the place where their canoe was anchored. They went aboard and paddled. Qā′teᵋnats said that they would go to an island called Egg Island.

Then his younger brother steered towards the island. They had not gone far when daylight came, and they were halfway across on their way to Egg Island. Then they saw a large (head of) kelp (standing) on the water, and Qā′teᵋnats at once asked his younger brother to steer for the kelp. His younger brother obeyed him at once. As soon as they arrived at the kelp, Qā′teᵋnats took hold of it and spoke to his younger brother. He said, "O brother! take care! I will climb down this kelp (stem) and see the world beneath us. Go home and arise early every morning and walk on the long beach, looking for me. Don't feel unhappy. Go home, brother." Thus he said, while he went into the water at the bow of the canoe, climbing down the kelp (stem). His younger brother went home at once.

Qā′teᵋnats had not gone very deep (down) when he came to the roof of a house through which the large seaweed was growing. As soon as Qā′teᵋnats arrived on the roof of the house, he heard some one in the house saying, "Go and see what makes the boards of the roof move." Thus he heard some one say. At once a man came to the place where Qā′teᵋnats was standing. The man said, "Come, Qā′teᵋnats, I am sent by the chief to invite you in." Thus he said to him. Qā′teᵋnats followed the man at once and entered the house. Then Qā′teᵋnats saw many people assembled, trying to cure a sick person; but none of the shamans could get the sickness of the sick person. Qā′teᵋnats saw a really stout man lying on his back in his seat. That was the chief Wealthy (Q!ō′mogwaᵋē).

Qā′teᵋnats was questioned at once; and a man said to him, "Oh, my dear! are you a shaman, that you may cure our friend, for he is really sick? None of the shamans can find (the cause of) his sickness." Thus he said to him. Qā′teᵋnats said at once that he was a great shaman, and the chief at once called to feel of him (for his sickness). As soon as Qā′teᵋnats went to him he saw the piece of bark lying flat on the side of the man who was lying down. As soon as Qā′teᵋnats had discovered the piece of bark, he recognized it as the same that he had thrown at the river where he had been purifying in the evening. The shamans did not see the piece of bark (lying there) that was the cause of the man's lying sick in the house. Behold! he was the double-headed serpent.

He put his hand on the bark, and the man screamed. Qā′teᵋnats pretended that there was difficulty in sucking out (the sickness) from his side. Three times he tried in vain to suck it out. Then the fourth time he took the bark and hid it, and the man got well at once. Then the serpent-man sat up and spoke to Qā'te⁽ᵋ⁾nats. He said, "Oh, my dear Qā'te⁽ᵋ⁾nats! you will be a very great shaman. You shall see now what supernatural gift you will obtain from me." Thus he said when the supernatural power came to Qā'te⁽ᵋ⁾nats. As soon as the supernatural power came into the house, a pond appeared (in the house), and reed matting was growing in the pond. A petrel came soaring over it; and as soon as Qā'te⁽ᵋ⁾nats came to his senses, the pond and the reed matting and the petrel disappeared.

Then he was sent home by the serpent-man. He went along under water and arrived home. His younger brother was walking along the long beach all the time. After Qā'te⁽ᵋ⁾nats had been away for four days, his younger brother started again in the morning, and found his elder brother lying dead at high-water mark. As soon as his younger brother reached him, Qā'te⁽ᵋ⁾nats awoke. They went to purify themselves; and as soon as they had finished, he tried his shaman's power. At once the pond came, the reed matting grew in it, and the petrel also came soaring over it. Soon he finished. Then he waited until evening; and as soon as it was evening, he sent his younger brother to go and make a fire in the house of his father. As soon as the fire was built in the house of his father, his younger brother invited his tribe in. As soon as they were all in, Qā'te⁽ᵋ⁾mo entered, who was the first shaman. Then that great shaman, Qā'te⁽ᵋ⁾nats entered. At once the pond appeared, with the reed matting, and the petrel soaring over it. Then he cured the sick among his tribe. Qā'te⁽ᵋ⁾mo did not believe that Qā'te⁽ᵋ⁾nats was a real shaman: therefore he lied and said that he was sick; and he begged Qā'te⁽ᵋ⁾nats to feel of his belly (for his sickness). Qā'te⁽ᵋ⁾nats at once discovered that he was lying, and therefore he tore his intestines, his liver, his lungs, and his heart to pieces. As soon as they were all broken up and mixed, he pulled them out of Qā'te⁽ᵋ⁾mo's anus.* Thus he killed Qā'te⁽ᵋ⁾mo. Now he had obtained what he had wished for when he went to purify in the river; and he continued to heal the sick among his people, and the pond and the reed matting and the petrel always appeared when he was healing. That is the end.

*Since this episode described is a physical impossibility, it confirms the metaphorical nature of myth. This imaginative and horrifying event rivets attention on a situation *turned inside out* by a clash between contending shamans. The legend may refer to an unresolved problem in society, i.e., that there is no satisfactory solution to the orderly succession of shamans where both have received power from the same supernatural and legitimate source.

Franz Boas and George Hunt, *Kwakiutl Texts*. Jesup North Pacific Expedition, vol. 10 (1906), pp. 22–27.

Appendix 5

Two Versions of the Origin of the Xwē′ xwe Dance.

Told by Yā′qoLas. Wä′qēᵋ was paddling about near Xŭlkᵘ. He went up northward until he came to K!wā′nēᵋ. There he went ashore, unloaded his canoe and stayed there for a long time. He built a small house there. One evening when he was sitting in the house he heard a rumbling noise and the talking of people. Then he purified himself because he thought that this was something supernatural. He heard it again and he went on to look for it. He came to A̧x̱ᵘdE′m and saw a house. Sparks were flying out through the roof. The noise came from this house. Suddenly it stopped and he heard people talking. He looked through a knot hole and saw the Xwē′ xwe dancing. When a certain word was pronounced in the song they fell down and were transformed into red cod. Their tails struck the ground and made the noise. They must have been secular because they did not notice when a stranger approached them. For four nights he went to look at their dance. Then he thought, "I am going in to see what they are doing." He went

Plate 43
X̌ʷi x̌ʷi *dancer at potlatch. Courtesy* Campbell River Courier

in. Nobody took notice of him. Then he stood up and said, "I have obtained you as my supernatural treasure. I want you for my supernatural dance." They agreed. The following is their song which is in a foreign language:

Hayamēnä yeheheya yeheheya nōgwaᵉm
hayamēnä yeheheya yeheheya memeqeya yeheya

Told by Lā'bit in 1912

Wä'qēᵉ was living at Xŭlkᵘ. Then he wished to paddle at sea to Trail-ahead-of-inlet (Ts!ē'qŭmēᵉ) and to see the place where Q!ā'neqeᵉlakᵘ had come down. And so he started paddling in the morning. And so it was evening when he came at Whale Beach Gwē'gwak·awaᵉlis and he hauled up his canoe. Then he built a house. And so as soon as he had finished building his house he went in and built a fire when it was getting dark. Then he ate after his arrival. And so as soon as he had finished Wä'qēᵉ lay down and tried to sleep. Then he could not go to sleep, for something was troubling him with troubles. And so it was late at night when he was startled by a rumbling sound that was heard by him. Then the floor of his house was shaking as in an earthquake. But it did not last long before it became quiet. Then he heard the rumbling sound; then the floor of his house shook again. Then it was that way four times. Then Wä'qēᵉ arose, went out of his house and sat down on the ground in front of his house. Then he heard a sound of many people talking at ȦxᵘdE'm on the north side of his house. Then Wä'qēᵉ went into his house and lay down on his bed. And he heard plainly the sound of many people talking. Then he went to sleep. Then he dreamt of a man who came into his house and said to him, "Don't sleep, friend, but go and purify yourself and wash with hemlock branches in this river and try to get tomorrow night what was heard by you. You will go again into the water in this river when daylight will first come in the morning; and so, as soon as it gets dark you will go and sit down on the ground inland from ȦxᵘdE'm; and so, as soon as the ground was quaked four times go into the winter ceremonial house and sit down at the right hand side inside the door. Don't be afraid," said the man as he went out. And so immediately Wä'qēᵉ arose and went to the river and broke off hemlock branches and sat down in the water in the river and rubbed his body with hemlock branches. And so as soon as he finished he went into his house and went to sleep. And so as soon as daylight came in the morning he went to the river and was sitting in the water while he was rubbing his body with hemlock branches. And so as soon as he had done so he entered his house and lay down on his bed and went to sleep when it was daylight. Then he dreamt of a man who came into his house. Then the man spoke to him. Then he said, "I come again, friend Wä'qēᵉ to tell you that there is no reason to fear us; and just go right into our winter ceremonial house tonight, when the fire in the middle of the house is not (yet) built, and sit down at the right hand side of the door; for you have really succeeded in purifying yourself immediately when I told you last night to go and sit in this river and to rub your body with hemlock branches," said the man as he went out of the house. And Wä'qēᵉ never ate that day. And so, as soon as it was evening he went into the river and sat in the water and rubbed his body with hemlock branches. And so, as soon as he had finished he started to go to ȦxᵘdE'm. And so, as soon as he had arrived at the cleared ground he sat down among the bushes. And so he had not been sitting there very long before it came to be dark. Then Wä'qēᵉ saw a large house built on the ground seaward from him, and there was no fire on the floor. Then Wä'qēᵉ arose from the ground at the place where he was sitting on the ground and went into the doorway of the house and he sat down on the right hand side inside the door. And Wä'qēᵉ did not hear one man walking about in the house. Then he saw glowing coals. Then (the fire) blazed up in the middle of the house. Then came many men and women walking in; and the men sat down in the rear of the house, and the women sat down on the sides of the house. And so as soon as all had sat down on the floor a man came in and stood on the floor in the rear of the house. He was the

speaker of the house. Then he spoke. Then he said, "We have all come in, supernatural
ones, now take care when the supernatural power comes to you, women, for I'll call
it," said he as he sang the sacred song which said:

> ᵋā ᵋā hā ᵋā ᵋā hā
> Magic spirit,
> ᵋā ᵋā hā ᵋā ᵋā hā
> Magic spirit,

said as he ran around the fire in the middle of the house reaching the place from which
he had come. Then all the women became red codfish and kicked about. That made
the rumbling noise all over the ground. But it was not very long before they turned
again into women, those who had been red codfish. Then the speaker of the house sang
his sacred song again, the same again as he had sung first. And so, as soon as it was again
ended, the women turned into red codfish and kicked about. Then he had done so four
times, when four men came into the door of the house, on their faces xwē' xwe masks.
They had long tongues and eyes standing out of the xwē' xwe masks. And four times
they went around the fire in the middle of the house walking with quick steps, and
those who were now red cod women just kept on kicking about while the four xwē'
xwe went with quick steps around the fire in the middle of the house. And so, as soon
as they had gone around four times the song leaders sang their songs, which said:

> Hāᵋyamena ye ne he ya ye he hê ya hāᵋyamena
> ye he he yā ye he he ya ye he ya he he
> Hāᵋyamena ye he he ya he I am hāᵋyamena
> ye he he ya ye he he ya he I am hāᵋyamena

And the four xwē' xwe danced carrying in each hand the scallop shells strung on a ring
of cedar withes. And so as soon as the song was at an end the song leaders sang again
one song which said:

> Go away, ugly ones, go away ugly ones, ha ha ha ha haa
> Ha, ugly ones with lolling tongues, ugly ones with lolling
>   tongues ha ha ha ha haa
> Ha, ugly ones with protruding eyes, ugly ones with
>   protruding eyes ha ha ha ha haa.

And the xwē' xwe danced around the fire in the middle of the house and they danced
out of the door. And the singing stopped after this and all the red codfish turned into
women again in the house and they sat down on the floor. Then the speaker of the
house spoke. Then he said, "O friends, now you have done well for this one who came
here to sit among us, our great friend Wä'qēᵋ. Now you have obtained as supernatural
treasure this great ceremonial, the xwē' xwe, for I am the Red Cod and this is my
house which has black sealions as the carvings of the four posts. Now you will have the
name Wä'qēᵋ, friend. What are you going to do with this house? Do you wish it to remain here or do you wish to go to Xŭlkᵘ where you come from?" said he. Then Wä'qēᵋ
said to him, "Thank you, friends, I really got a supernatural treasure. In the past could
not be seen the great ceremonial, the xwē' xwe and this winter ceremonial house, for I
wish this house to be on the ground of my village site Xŭlkᵘ," said Wä'qēᵋ. Then said
the speaker of the house, "Now go, friend Wä'qēᵋ. Go home tomorrow morning. I and
my tribe will follow you after four days. Your house will be taken and put up where
you wish the house to be put on the ground in the night when I arrive. And so, as soon
as the house will be finished I will tell you, and go at once and call your tribe that all
may go into this house to sit down on both lower sides of the house in this manner and
I will sit at the upper end of the house, and you will stand at the place where I stand in

the rear of the house when you sing my sacred song for calling (the spirits), for you will not see me and my tribe, for we shall be invisible when we come," said he. Then Wä'qēᵋ said, "Now I will go home in the morning and I shall be expecting you. Thank you for your words, friend," said he as the fire in the middle of the house disappeared. Then all the men and women and the house disappeared. Wä'qēᵋ just went back to his house and slept a little while. And so, as soon as it got daylight in the morning he started by canoe and so it was not yet evening when he arrived at Xŭlkᵘ, and so he went right into his house and lay down on his bed. Now he was lying down for four days. And so, as soon as he had stayed in the house four days he arose early in the morning to invite his whole tribe with women and children to go and eat breakfast in his house. And so, as soon as they had all come in, Wä'qēᵋ gave them food, and so, as soon as they had finished eating Wä'qēᵋ spoke. Then he said, "Welcome, tribe, and all of you listen to what will be my word to you, for I wish all of you to go into the water of this river today. Don't ask me what I mean, just guess it," said he. And so immediately his whole tribe went out of the house and went into the water in the river while Wä'qēᵋ also went into the water in the river and rubbed his body with hemlock branches. And his tribe guessed that he had obtained a supernatural treasure where he had been. And so, as soon as the whole tribe had washed themselves Wä'qēᵋ said to his tribe, "O tribe! now you are ready for what I am expecting tonight. Take care and stand up right away when I call you; and that, do not be afraid of what will be heard by you, tribe," said Wä'qēᵋ to his tribe. And so, as soon as it was evening the whole tribe was ready, and so as soon as it was dark in the night Wä'qēᵋ heard whispering which said, "Come, friend Wä'qēᵋ, and go into your house," said it. And so immediately Wä'qēᵋ followed what was only heard walking; for he did not see a person. They went into the house and there were only glowing coals in the fire in the middle of the house. Then the noise of talking asked Wä'qēᵋ to invite his tribe, that all should come in. And so, immediately Wä'qēᵋ invited his tribe. And so all came in and sat down on the floor at the lower sides of both sides of the house. Then Wä'qēᵋ stood up in the rear of the house. Then he said to his tribe, "Now come, tribe, and look at my supernatural treasure," said he as he sang the sacred song of the speaker of the house. And so, as soon as the sacred song was ended, there was a rumbling sound on both sides of the house and the floor was shaking. But it was not very long before the rumbling sound stopped. Then also the shaking of the floor became quiet. Then it was awhile before Wä'qēᵋ sang again the sacred song. And so, as soon as the sacred song was at an end there was again a rumbling sound and the floor was shaking as in an earthquake. Three times it did so. But that was now the fourth time when the four xwē' xwe masks came. Their song was sung by the invisible ones and the four xwē' xwe danced. And so, as soon as the song was ended their other song was sung. Then the four xwē' xwe danced again and danced into the bedroom. Now they finished. And Wä'qēᵋ spoke. Then he said, "O tribe, now you have seen the supernatural treasure which I received from the Red Cod and the great winter ceremonial house with the carved posts which are black sealions," said he as he went into the bedroom. And he saw the four xwē' xwe masks and four large drums and also four notched round cedar poles, one fathom long; and that, the four scallop shells strung on a ring of cedar withes which are carried by the xwē' xwe when they are dancing. These were put into the room, for there is no food and property that was obtained as a treasure by Wä'qēᵋ from the Red Cod. That is the reason why it is said that the red codfish are stingy. And that is the end.

Franz Boas, *Kwakiutl Tales* (1935).

Plate 44
From a painting entitled ''Southeast
Wind'' by We-Wai-Kum artist Mark
Henderson. Courtesy of the artist

Appendix 6

Most-Beautiful-One, excerpts from a We-Wai-Kum tale

Some of the Lē'gwiłdax^u say that the princesses of Down-Dancer were singing love-songs all the time, naming Most-Beautiful-One. For that reason our lord, Most-Beautiful-One, wished to go to the place where they lived. Soon he arrived at PenL!ats. Then he borrowed the (devil-fish) mask of the Devil-Fish. As soon as he obtained the devil-fish mask, he put it on. Then he sat on the ground; and he had not sat there long when he heard the princesses of Down-Dancer coming and singing love-songs about Most-Beautiful-One. Then Most-Beautiful-One saw that she who came first was the eldest one. As soon as the eldest one saw the old man, she picked up stones and threw them at him. The two younger sisters did the same. The youngest one was far behind her three elder sisters: therefore she came after the elder ones had thrown stones at the old man. As soon as she saw the old man, she took pity on him. Then she went to him, and the girl spoke to the old man. Then her elder sisters left her, and afterwards Most-Beautiful-One showed himself. Then the girl sent him behind the house, and Most-Beautiful-One obeyed her words. Then he took off his (devil-fish) mask, and took it back to the Devil-Fish. Afterward he again went behind the house; and so the youngest princess of Down-Dancer always went into the woods, although she had never done so before, for indeed she had Most-Beautiful-One secretly for her husband. Then Down-Dancer guessed that his youngest daughter secretly had a husband (man); for as soon as day came in the morning, the princess would go into the woods, and she would come home only when it grew dark in the evening. After two months had passed, Down-Dancer (secretly) asked his three daughters to secretly follow their youngest sister to see where she always went in the woods. In the morning, as soon as day came, the youngest daughter went away, and the three elder ones followed her secretly. They had not gone far into the woods when they heard their youngest sister playing with a man, and they just went right to the place where the youngest sister was. Then they saw their youngest sister sitting on the ground with a really handsome young man. Then the three women went to them and sat on the ground also; and they began to play with their younger sister. They had forgotten that they were sent to watch the youngest one. Then they all fell in love with him whom they had seen, and they discovered that it was he who is named Most-Beautiful-One whom they had seen. Then in the evening they were sent home by Most-Beautiful-One, and they went home. And the three women did so also for two months.

Then Down-Dancer really felt badly on account of his youngest daughter, for she had done so now for four months. Then he scolded his four princesses in vain. The four children only disobeyed him. Therefore Down-Dancer threatened to kill the husband of his princesses if he should find him. . . .

The three elder sisters of the young woman continued to go in vain into the woods, looking for the place where Most-Beautiful-One had been before; and therefore Down-Dancer always threatened the man who was turning the heads of his daughters. That is what made Most-Beautiful-One feel badly on account of his (secret) father-in-law.

After a long time, Down-Dancer got ready to paddle in his canoe to look after his deer-nets at the island in front of PenL!ats, which is named Denman Island. (That is what our ancestors used for catching deer.) Then Down-Dancer wished to take the old man to look after his canoe when he should go out of the canoe into the woods. As soon as the old man had gone aboard, they began to paddle. Then they arrived at Denman Island. Then Down-Dancer stepped out of his canoe, and he saw five deer caught in his net. He took them out at once; and as soon as the five deer had been taken out, he carried them to the beach. When he arrived at the place where his canoe was, he saw a really handsome man sitting in the stern of the canoe; and as soon as Down-Dancer saw him, the man went out to sea, and the canoe was far from the rocks (of the beach). Then Down-Dancer wondered about the man. He saw now that the one who was sitting in the canoe was not like a common man. Then he tried to call him. He said, "Come ashore, my dear, that I may put my game into the canoe!" Thus he said in vain; but the man only shook his body, and therefore the canoe went farther out to sea. Then Down-Dancer became frightened because he was aware that (the man in the canoe) was not a common man. The reason of his fear was that the island on which he staid was really not large. Therefore he thought that he would give the oldest of his princesses to the man. He said to him, "Oh, my dear! I will give you the oldest of my princesses if you will come (that you may come) and take me aboard." The man only shook his body, and the canoe went still farther out. Then Down-Dancer became really scared, and he shouted again, and said, "Oh, my dear, come and take me aboard! You shall have the next oldest of my princesses for your wife." Thus he tried to say again; but the man only shook his body again, and the canoe went still farther out. Then Down-Dancer shouted again, and said again, "Oh, my dear! I will give you my third daughter for a wife. Come and take me aboard!" Thus he tried to say; but the man only did the same as he had done before. Now Down-Dancer could hardly see him, for he was very far away. Then Down-Dancer was really frightened; and he said, "Come, take me aboard! You shall have the youngest of my princesses for a wife." Thus he said to him.

At once the canoe came to the beach where Down-Dancer was standing. Then Down-Dancer saw that the source of the brilliant light (that proceeded from) the man was his abalone (sic) earrings. As soon as the canoe came to the beach, Down-Dancer put the five deer aboard the canoe, and Down-Dancer also went aboard. In vain Down-Dancer took his paddle and tried to paddle. He was forbidden by the handsome man to paddle. He was told, "Only watch me." Then the body of the man shook, and that made the canoe start. Then Down-Dancer was startled, for his canoe had reached the beach of his house.

Then he was met by his three eldest daughters; and last came the youngest one, who was secretly married to our lord. As soon as the three princesses of Down-Dancer saw our lord sitting in the stern of the canoe, they tried to get ahead of each other in reaching him; but our lord did not take any notice of them at all. The youngest one arrived, and at once our lord went out of the canoe and put his arm around her waist, and they went up from the beach immediately and entered the house of his father-in-law. Therefore Down-Dancer felt very badly, and he already hated his son-in-law. (This is the beginning of the hate between son-in-law and father-in-law.)

Now she had been married for a long time to our lord. Then Down-Dancer became sick. He scolded in the house, and said, "That I should have a man of supernatural power for my son-in-law and still have no firewood to warm myself!" As soon as he stopped speaking, our lord, Most-Beautiful-One, arose and went out of the house. He went to a thick pinetree which stood at one end of the village (site) and pushed it over. As soon as the tree fell, he pulled the wood out from the bark, and only the bark was lying on the ground. This our lord carried on his shoulder; and when he arrived, he threw it down outside of his father-in-law's house. Then Down-Dancer's tribe tried in vain to take the bark away. It did not grow less, although they were taking from it throughout the winter. Then Down-Dancer discovered that his son-in-law was a man of supernatural power. Therefore he tried in vain to devise some other wish.

Then it occurred to him to ask his son-in-law to pick salmon-berries, for he knew that winter was a season when there weren't any. In vain he tried to disconcert our lord. Immediately our lord asked his wife for a small basket; and as soon as it was given to him, he went out into the woods. It was not very long before he came carrying in his hand a small basket full of salmon-berries, and then he gave them to his father-in-law. Down-Dancer thought the salmon-berries (were not enough for him), for he wished to use them to give a feast to his tribe. Then Most-Beautiful-One felt worse (than before) on account of his father-in-law; and he said to him, "O father-in-law! go on, invite your tribe, and try to use them up." Thus he said. Down-Dancer at once sent his four attendants to invite his tribe to come and eat salmon-berries. They all went at once; and it was not long before the people came into the house. Then many dishes were taken, and salmon-berries were put into them, and the salmon-berries in the small basket did not grow any less. Then they were put before the tribe of Down-Dancer, and our lord was praised on account of what he had done. Now, Down-Dancer was really jealous of his son-in-law because he was praised by his tribe on account of the salmon-berries, which were constantly getting more.

Therefore Down-Dancer again devised another wish. He said, "O son-in-law! go and get what I am wishing for; namely, two woodpeckers, which shall come and pick off the insects from my house." Thus he said. Our lord at once went out of the house of his father-in-law. He went into the woods, and it was not long before he came into the house bringing two woodpeckers. Then our lord whispered to the woodpeckers, "Don't stop pecking the whole day and the whole night." Thus he said to them. Then they were given to his father-in-law. Down-Dancer at once took the two woodpeckers and let them fly. When the two woodpeckers had flown away, they sat down, each in one corner of the house, and they began to peck; and they did not rest the whole day, nor even the whole night. Down-Dancer became tired of them, and asked his son-in-law to send them out. Then Most-Beautiful-One felt badly because his father-in-law troubled him so much, and therefore Most-Beautiful-One told the woodpeckers to peck Down-Dancer to death. Then the two birds pecked at him and between them killed Down-Dancer.

As soon as Down-Dancer was dead, Most-Beautiful-One spoke to his wife, and said, "O mistress! what has been done by the birds to your father was not my wish, for the birds just got tired of him because he troubled them so much. That is all. Now I shall also leave you," said our lord, and disappeared. That is the end.

Some people say that Most-Beautiful-One threw the old-man mask into the water at Denman Island when Down-Dancer went into the woods to look after his deer-net, and therefore there are many devil-fish at Denman Island.

Franz Boas and George Hunt. *Kwakiutl Texts* (1906).

Appendix 7

Lament of the Nobles

Your spirit is now travelling around
the Mortal World, my Noble
Are you not?
You are now travelling to a great
distant world, my Noble,
Are you not?
You are now travelling to a great
distant world, my Noble,
Are you not?
Your many talents we were fortunate
to have my Noble, will be a great loss
Um Humy My Yah, Yah

You are now walking to a great
world, my Noble,
Are you not?
You are walking to a great
world, my Noble,
Are you not?
Your many talents we were fortunate
to have my Noble, will be a great loss
Um Humy My Yah, Yah

You are now flying to this great world, my Noble,
Are you not?
You are now flying to this great world, my Noble,
Your many talents we were fortunate
to have my Noble, will be a great loss.
Um Humy My Yah, Yah

You are now going it disappear into
that distant world, my Noble,
Are you not?
You are now going to disappear into
that distant world, my Noble,
Are you not?
Your many talents we were fortunate
to have my Noble, will be a great loss.
Um Humy My Yah, Yah

You are now going to remain in that
great world, my Noble,
Are you not?
You are now going to remain in that
great world, my Noble,
Are you not?
Your many talents we were fortunate
to have my Noble, will be a great loss
Um Humy My Yah, Yah
Your Spirit is travelling around the
Spirit World, my Noble.
Are you not?

Daisy Sewid-Smith, by permission of James Sewid.
Campbell River Salmon Festival Souvenir Booklet, 1973.

Appendix 8

The Welcome Pole

This is the pole to welcome the people. It comes from Rivers Inlet. Chief Walkus* gave the pole to Johnny Dick's father as part of a dowry.

Once upon a time this man was going up the River Wanukw. He had a servant paddling his canoe. The man's name was Ow'emgu'emgela. The name of the village he was going to was called Nuxwens. While he was going up the river he saw one smoke. (Smoke from one house.) All the other houses were empty. He approached the house where he saw the smoke and then went ashore.

Ow'emgu'emgela and his servant went inside the house. They saw one old lady near the fire but they did not say anything to her. They sat on the opposite side of the fire.

Ow'emgu'emgela discovered that the old lady was totally blind for she was groping her way around. She was feeling for her cooking utensils and food. Ow'emgu'emgela teased the old lady by hiding her food. She was still unaware that the men were in her house. The old lady shouted towards a room behind her. She called her granddaughter to come and find the food she was looking for.

Then this beautiful young girl came out. The girl said, "The two men sitting opposite you must have taken it."

The old lady invited the girl to come out and share a meal with the two men. The beautiful girl came out and ate with the strangers. They were eating whale meat.

When they had finished the meat, Ow'emgu'emgela said to his servant, "Go fetch me some water from the river."

The old lady said to Ow'emgu'emgela. "Don't send your servant. You will notice the village is empty. There is a huge river-monster that swallowed all my people when they went near the river."

Ow'emgu'emgela took off his Sisiutl belt and put it on his servant. They all watched the servant go to the river's edge. The river-monster came and swallowed him.

Ow'emgu'emgela called out, "Break apart! Break apart! Break apart!" He was telling the Sisiutl to break open the river-monster. The river-monster jumped onto the shore and his stomach broke apart.

The servant escaped from the stomach. Human bones spilled out on the shore as well as human beings that were still half alive.

Ow'emgu'emgela took the water of life and splashed it on the half-living people. They were revived and returned to their homes.

Ow'emgu'emgela gave the old lady sight by splashing the water of life on her eyes. She was very grateful and showed her appreciation by giving the beautiful young girl to Ow'emgu'emgela.

The Sisiutl on the Welcome Pole commemorates the Sisiutl that Ow'emgu'emgela put on his servant to save the servant and kill the river-monster.

Courtesy Kwagiulth Museum at Cape Mudge.

*Wakius of Alert Bay is known to the public through the unveiling of the new "Wakas Totem Pole" in Stanley Park, Vancouver in May 1987, under the auspices of The Canadian Museum of Civilization, et al. His portrait appears on p. 91 of *Prosecution or Persecution* by Daisy Sewid-Smith, with the information that he was arrested in the Village Island potlatch of 1921.

Appendix 9
Descendants of Harry and Ida Assu

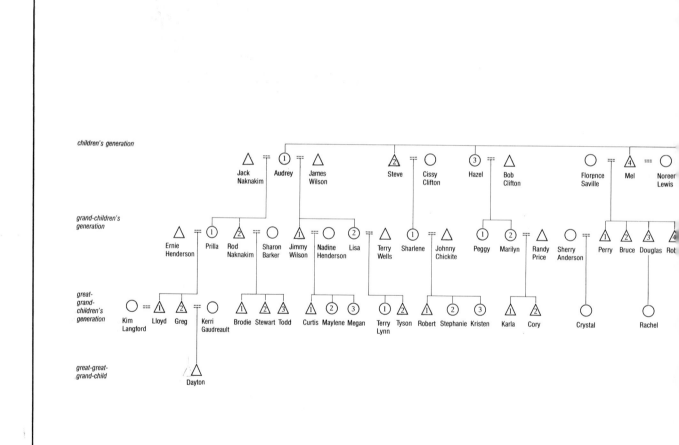

153

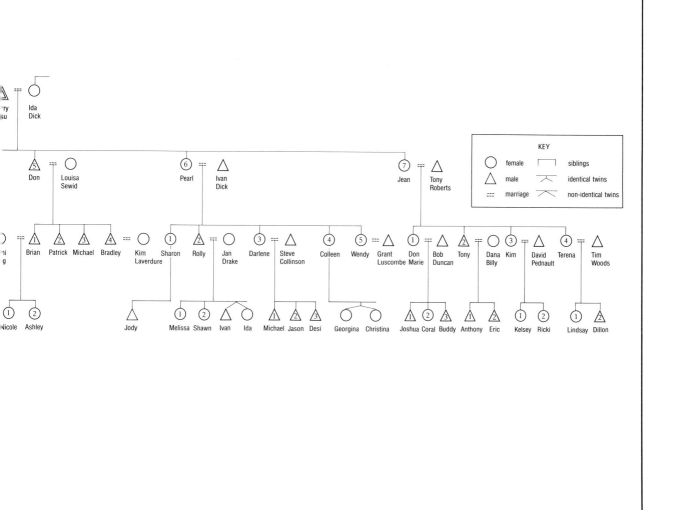

KEY

○ female   ☐ siblings

△ male   ⋈ identical twins

=== marriage   ⋎ non-identical twins

Appendix 10

Duntsik Power Board from Cape Mudge

The spirit represented in Kwagiulth power boards is the Sisiutl, the double-headed serpent of the sea.*

The board was shown during winter dances, especially by the society initiating youth into the ritual of Winalagilis, the warrior spirit.

The power board portrays the Sisiutl rising up among the people gathered in the big house. It rose slowly out of the earth floor, swaying and glittering in the firelight to the great awe of the assembly.

The Duntsik board was used in the performance of the Tokwit, a woman of great magic powers derived from the Sisiutl. She conjures the two-headed serpent to appear before the people, claiming to control its death-dealing power. Often the performance by the Tokwit dancer calls for her to be slain by the monster in the form of the Duntsik board, subsequently to return to life demonstrating her greater power.

In some performances the Tokwit dancer seizes the horns of the Sisiutl as the board emerges from the floor and is then dragged underground as it submerges. Her attendants, struggling to save her life, are buried underground with her. Four days later the powers conferred upon her to overcome the Sisiutl are demonstrated by their miraculous return to life.

Courtesy Kwagiulth Museum, Cape Mudge.

*This account is associated with the "Duntsik" or power board on display in the Kwagiulth Museum, Cape Mudge. The board as shown in the photograph on p. 41 was a gift of the National Museum of Canada to the museum at the time of Opening, June 1979. It was formerly in the Museum of the American Indian Heye Foundation and was collected by G. G. Heye from the village of Cape Mudge in 1908. Ownership now determined.

Sources

Barnett, Homer
    1955 *The Coast Salish Indians of British Columbia.* Eugene: University of Oregon Press

Barbeau, Marius
    1950 *Totem Poles.* Vol. 2, Ottawa. National Museum of Canada

Boas, Franz
    1887 "Zur Ethnologie British-Kolumbiens," *Peterman's Geography.* Mitteilungen, Germany, Pp. 129–33
    1897 "The Social Organization and Secret Societies of the Kwakiutl Indians." Report of the U.S. National Museum for 1895. Washington, D.C.: Smithsonian Institution
    1921 "Ethnology of the Kwakiutl." 35th Annual Report, Bureau of Ethnology, Smithsonian Institution. New York: reprinted by AMS Press, 1969
    1935 *Kwakiutl Tales*, New Series. Columbia University Contributions to Anthropology, Vol. 25, part I. New York: Columbia University Press

Boas, F., and Hunt, George
    1906 *Kwakiutl Texts.* Second Series: "Traditions of the Legwiłdaʔxʷ." Vol. 10. Jesup North Pacific Expedition

Codere, Helen
    1950 *Fighting with Property.* Monographs of the American Ethnological Society, no. 18. New York: J. J. Augustin

Curtis, Edward
    1915 *The North American Indian.* Vol 10. *The Kwakiutl.* Nordwood: Plimpton Press

Drucker, Paul
    Circa 1953 Unpublished field notes. Manuscript No. 4516 (2). Vol. 6. National Anthropological Archives, Smithsonian Institution, Washington, D.C. Interview with Chief Billy Assu on history, social organization, potlatches

Drucker, P., and Heizer, R.
    1967 *To Make My Name Good: A Re-Examination of the Kwakiutl Potlatch.* Berkeley and Los Angeles: University of California Press

Duff, Wilson
    circa 1960 "Southern Kwakiutl." Unpublished field notes. Courtesy Kwakiutl District Council, Port Hardy, B.C.
    1965 *The Indian History of British Columbia: Vol. 1. The Impact of the White Man.* Memoir 5. Victoria: Provincial Museum

Duff, W., and Taylor, H.
       1956 "A Post-Contact Southward Movement of the Kwakiutl." Researc
            Studies 24 (1). Bellingham: Western Washington State College
Dawson, G. M.
       1887 "Notes and Observations on the Kwakiool People of the Northern Pa
            of Vancouver Island." Proceedings and Transactions of the Royal Socie
            of Canada for the year 1887, vol. 5, sec. 2. pp. 63–98.
Hawthorn, Audrey
       1979 *Kwakiutl Art*. Vancouver: Douglas and McIntyre
Inglis, Joy
       1964 "The Interaction of Myth and Social Context in the Village of Car
            Mudge." Master's thesis, UBC
Inglis, Stephen
       1979 "Cultural Readjustment: A Canadian Case Study." *Quarterly of the Co
            nadian Museums Association* 12, no. 3
Kennedy, D., and Bouchard, R.
       1983 *Sliammon Life, Sliammon Lands*. Vancouver: Talonbooks
       1988 "Northern Coast Salish" (in press). Northwest Volume of the Handboo
            of American Indians, Washington, D.C.: Smithsonian Institution
Kirk, Ruth
       1986 *Wisdom of the Elders*. Vancouver: Douglas and McIntyre and Royal Bri
            ish Columbia Museum
Macnair, Peter
       1977 "Kwakiutl Winter Dances: A Reenactment." Ottawa: Artscanada.
Mauzé, Marie
       1983 "The Potlatch Law and the Confiscation of Ceremonial Property amor
            the Kwakiutl." *Bulletin Amérique Indienne*
       1984 *Enjeux et Jeux du prestige des Kwagul méridionaux aux Lekwiltoq (cô
            nord-ouest du Pacifique)*. Ph.d. dissertation, Ecole des Hautes Etudes e
            Sciences Sociales, Paris
Report of the Royal Commission on Indian Affairs for the Province of British Colun
       1916 bia, Vol. 3. Victoria: Provincial Archives
Skinner, Mark
       1986 "Analysis of Human Skeletal Remains. Site: Cape Mudge Villag
            Quadra Island, B.C. (EaSh3)." Report to Heritage Conservation Branc
            Government of British Columbia, Victoria
Sewid-Smith, Daisy
       1979 *Prosecution or Persecution*. Nu-Yum-Balees Society. Cape Mudg
            Kwagiulth Museum

Index